Reconnection

a memoir

Lucas A Catton

ISBN: 978-0-578-63310-7

DEDICATION

To Leslie, Ella, Rhett and Max. My world.

CONTENTS

ACKNOWLEDGMENTS

Thank you to everyone who has taken the time to share your story with me, whether privately or in public. It has helped give me the courage to write and publish this book.

INTRODUCTION

I struggled with writing this book for a few years, partially because I am not an accomplished author with crazy literary skills, but mainly because I kept thinking there was going to be some grand point I could make, reveal or reach in the end, although it never really happened. Looking back, that actually is the point. It never ends, until it does. The good, the bad, the irritating and the divine. The love, the sorrow, the joy, the pain, the ecstasy. This is living, and being willing to experience and connect with all that life has to offer, and to make the most out of all of these combined day to day events is the task at hand, with the mission to hopefully enhance the lives of those around us and leave the world a better place within our sphere of influence.

I believe that we can create the lives we want to live within our experiences and how we respond to them internally and externally. We can also choose to create new experiences, and new responses. When we don't, we are no longer living, but instead just existing in a state of reaction only to others and those external factors as a semi-willing participant, unaware that we are unaware.

Who am I? How do I describe myself or define who I am to others? Do I include my future dreams and goals along with my current activities? How much of my past do I reveal? What is the purpose of what I'm doing right now, and is it a worthwhile endeavor? These are questions that I often ponder.

Numerous times throughout any given day, week or month, I ask myself who I think I am, whether or not I'm living up to that identity and if I am moving through life in a positive manner contributing to others. Sometimes I overdo it and get down on myself for not doing enough. I do often feel like I should be accomplishing great things and then get disappointed if I don't think I'm making enough progress in a certain area or time frame. This can be something as simple as completing home improvement tasks or include writing projects and major career changes. This form of self-criticism can easily move from motivational over into self-shaming, which is detrimental to well-being.

Then I have to slow down, take a look around and realize how far I've come. I have gone through numerous shifts in identity throughout the years, but now I feel like I'm getting closer and closer to the real me inside, and that it has taken the entire batch of struggles and joys to make that progress.

What follows is a story of a part of my life as I have transformed through several major changes in recent years, and yet the entire thing is still just a blip on the radar of what I feel is continually evolving. I am a different person even from when I pushed "publish" to share this with anyone who chooses to read it. I have tried to be honest and lay bare my struggles and successes, and be grateful for all of them. Consciously reconnecting with myself, with others and the world around me is a challenge, and is also a deeply rewarding practice.

Although I am now in my forties, I still feel like I am at least ten years younger most of the time, just with less hair and hopefully a little more perspective and appreciation for life.

What I've found is that there is no perfect lesson or situation. Things could always be better or they could always be worse, but there are an infinite number of perfect moments, and strung together they can make life beautiful and very much worth living. Trying to wish things were different from a sense of lack or frustration only creates further discomfort, but accepting them as they are and moving on from there can set a foundation for positive change.

For as long as I can remember, I seemed to have had this underlying thought that I was an exception to the rule. I bucked against "the system" more times than I can count and proudly called myself a nonconformist, even if I didn't know what that meant when I was younger. Most often the result was that I became more free and confident in myself afterward, but there were also plenty of times that it proved to be a difficult way to go through life. Having this attitude is how I feel I have been able to attract many positive people, things and experiences, because I simply didn't accept that things are only supposed to be a certain way or follow certain rules. Even when I would find myself stuck in a rut of at-first-unintentional conformity to someone else's construct, I have been able to dig back out and regain some freedom again.

This is why I walked out of my AP English class in high school one day to change my course of studies. After I openly questioned the lesson being taught that day about a work of classic literature, my teacher had told me that my interpretation of the book was wrong, and that I just had to accept it as being wrong. I realized that they didn't actually want me to think freely, but to think the way they were teaching. I wasn't willing to keep going that route, and at that point decided I would rather enjoy my experience instead of push the limits of my high school education. Some would say that by not choosing the highest academic goals, I watered down my chances for success or career advancement, but I disagree.

It was also how I figured out that I could reduce my senior year to only half a day for half a year through selective engineering of my schedule, and still graduate with honors. It is how I wound up in managerial and executive positions at companies

I've worked for, even when I had little to no prior experience starting in my teens, and why I've also been successfully self employed for more than a dozen years and started multiple seven-figure companies. To be fair, it has certainly been a force in many of my failures and less than stellar performances as well.

Additionally, this character trait has been a huge factor in how I got into some difficult situations, including many of the ones in this book. Sometimes I refused to go along with what everyone else was doing if I wasn't satisfied with the answers I was getting. There were plenty of times where I could have just walked away quietly without making a bigger deal, but I felt at the time that the opposition message should at least be heard. I hope that doesn't translate into me being a confrontational person. I like to think of it is challenging, in a mostly positive way, or an advocate for more informed consent. Nonetheless, I still consider this a very valuable asset, and I intend on always questioning things as they are, in search for higher meaning and deeper understanding.

1. CULT SURVIVOR GETS A SECOND CHANCE AT LIFE

Yes, that's me.

A few years ago I wrote a book about my time in Scientology and one of its organizations called Narconon. After a few months I pulled it from distribution because I didn't want those darker moments of my life to define me. I felt that my purposes for writing it had been largely accomplished, but there is also more to be told since then. In some ways, I realized that I can't escape that part of my life completely (as Google reminds me any time I search my name), and that instead I needed to continue telling my story as it unfolds. I believe that all that I've been through is relevant to my evolving future, and that I've learned so much in the process.

Splashy headlines about celebrities leaving Scientology have certainly become more common in recent years, and more people like me have been empowered to share their experiences as well. This book isn't about Scientology, though, it's about reemerging from the pits of despair and having a better life. It's about finding hope and meaning despite the temporary hopeless chaos. Even though I never felt like I was in physical danger, my mental health definitely suffered during the time leading up to my exit and for a few years after. In a sense, I suppose I'm still recovering in some ways. There have been many ex-members who weren't able to make it out so lucky in the end, and several who have taken their own lives as a result. I am grateful to have had the support that I did and to have held on to the dream of turning things around.

A lot of people who hear about Scientology now wonder how someone could get sucked into that these days, but my initial introduction really started prior to the year 2000, so most of the negative information wasn't as easily found online compared to the ample amount of content readily available now. It wasn't in the mainstream media, either, but instead there were commercials running for *Dianetics* on television. But what was the draw? Well, it would be easy to say that my parents were involved at the time and they sent me to Narconon because I was aimless and drinking too much as a teenager and young adult. While true, blaming them wouldn't be fair or fully accurate (they are no longer a part of it either). It had more to do with my challenging nature and an inherent desire to belong somewhere.

From a very young age I remember feeling like I had out of body experiences, extra-sensory perceptions or some other undefined spiritual occurrences, and I believed that there was more out there than what I was learning on Sundays and reading from the Bible. I have very fond memories of my Presbyterian youth group activities and the community of families that gathered together, but the most spiritual moments were in connection with others believing in a force greater than ourselves - sort of an otherwise nameless identity that I had to accept as having a name and identity, according to the books we studied, hymns we sang and sermons we listened to. Although I went along with it, I found myself continually asking if there was more to it, and so I kept searching. I also had plenty of exposure through my extended family's Catholic upbringing and friends' families who were devout Baptists, as well as a few others sprinkled throughout the years.

Toward the end of high school I tried becoming a Mormon and was inducted to the LDS church. My girlfriend's family was part of that church, and I became interested in a storyline that had both parallels and differences to what I grew up with. I spent a lot of time with some Mormon missionary elders, and even got baptized into the church. By then I had been exposed to several versions of Christian faiths, but I still didn't feel like I really fit in with any of them. I was still searching for something, but I didn't know what.

So, my aimless irresponsibility wound up getting me to Narconon, where I found something I enjoyed - a group of people who were very raw and real and willing to discuss just about anything. Such openness was refreshing, and I made a bunch of friends who worked there and eventually decided to join them. I felt really excited about life again, working with a team of people who had a common purpose and who were willing to do whatever it took to achieve it. The stated purpose was to help people get off drugs, but the real purpose was of course to introduce them to L. Ron Hubbard so that they would hopefully continue studying and getting more involved in Scientology. It worked on me and totally played into my desire to go against the status quo.

For me, what was initially intriguing about Scientology was that really for the first time I felt there was a group of people and supposedly a path I could follow to get to know myself more mentally and spiritually, with the goal of becoming more free, and even "enlightened." The nuggets of helpful stuff that Hubbard took from other religions and therapies were enough to set the hook. However, through reading Hubbard's writings, listening to his lectures and going through spiritual counseling they called auditing, the real end result is people become a slave to his word and are taught to always refer back to him as "Source."

As I got deeper into it, I fell harder for each next carrot dangled in front of me saying that I was getting closer and closer to finding out the secrets of the Universe. Hubbard was a master manipulator, in that he forbid members at higher levels to reveal anything to members at lower levels, saying that they could actually get sick and maybe even die from the information and spiritual practices until they were ready to receive it. There was a ton of secrecy, and those who had done the higher levels had to pretend like they knew something special and were more enlightened. This then encouraged others to keep moving up (and giving more money, of course) and dedicating themselves more to the cause. Since nobody could talk about their "case" to each other or what they were auditing at these upper levels, nobody publicly admitted that it was hogwash, for fear of seeming like the only one who didn't have an amazing spiritual experience and the fear of possibly not getting to the next level. There were endless carrots dangled, and a chain of lies upheld through secrecy and strict adherence.

And so it continued. Deeper in, higher up, more involved, more secrets, more people pretending they were enlightened, more lies and manipulation from Hubbard. At the same time, I would often give credit to anything good in my life as being the result of my involvement and believed that anything bad was the result of not applying it correctly. Again, this was another thing that was taught. I bought into the idea that I was becoming more self-determined through it, when in actual fact I was giving up my self-determinism to the mandates of a man who was in my estimation deranged and a group who was pushing his agenda. For a time, I had given up the trait of questioning authority because I thought that being involved in this fringe group was doing just that.

Members were forbidden to read or watch anything negative about Hubbard or Scientology, and were punished for doing so when forced to go through confessionals. When I started to question things, reading stories about members who had defected and buck their system, I was of course also subjected to them. These confessionals, which were also sometimes called security checks, consisted of an interrogator sitting on the other side of a device called an e-meter, which is supposed to measure reactivity, and asking probing questions to see what kind of response was created. Once there was a response they would hone in on it until a satisfactory enough answer was given and there were no more indicators of troubled areas. Then they usually ended with questions that were looking to get further reactions to see if anything was missed. These were questions like, "Regarding this confessional, was anything missed?" or "In this confessional, have you told all?"

The amount of anxiety that builds up, on top of any shame or guilt of things that might be embarrassing, continues to mount. Sweaty palms, heart pounding, tense muscles and a feeling of being spiritually disemboweled. There were several times where I literally just wanted to scream and run out because I was being accused of things I didn't do, or being punished for not doing as I was told, and I just couldn't take it anymore. Instead, I had to put on a good show to calm myself down in order to prove that I wasn't hiding anything or failing to tell them something. It was torturous.

When people questioned Hubbard's teachings they were told that there must have been something they didn't understand or must have done something wrong. Even though most was written in the '50s and '60s and culturally inappropriate, to say the least, Hubbard was Source and people had to follow his directions exactly. That is how he got the group think cult mentality going, even claiming that they wouldn't make it into the next life in good shape if they didn't do as they were told. This whole time I kept going because I just knew there had to be something at the end that would answer some questions for me about my existence and the provide some amazing revelation. I desperately wanted to believe that all I had been through would lead me somewhere special. Instead, it's like a ladder to nowhere.

It's easy for someone else to say, "I never would have fallen for that bullshit." That may be true today since there has been so much exposure in the media, online and even in pop culture, in part because of other people like me - former members who became whistleblowers, but it's a different time now and circumstances are tough to understand if people haven't experienced the same things.

Through a period of more than a decade, I

primarily associated with other Scientologists. Most of my friendships and work activities involved people in that small group, all equally delusional in feeling we were the only ones who really knew all the answers to save mankind (think Tom Cruise in his infamous video posted in 2008 about Scientologists being the only ones who can help that sparked the Anonymous retaliation on Scientology).

My arrogance and blind allegiance eventually started to crack. I was sick of being asked for money all of the time and paying ridiculous prices to be made to feel like shit in the end. I was being mentally and spiritually dragged through hell and I couldn't make sense of it anymore. So I finally started to really look at what they didn't want me to look at - information about them from former members who exposed their practices and exposed the lies Hubbard told to his flock, and those of its current leader, David Miscavige. For the first time it finally started to make sense - that I wasn't the crazy one, they all were. Over the next year or so I started to regain my individual identity, and became less of a sheep, but I still had a very long way to go as I struggled to find a way out.

By then I was already going through a divorce and was trying to figure out how I could remain a constant figure in my daughter's life. I had hopes of a new start. I bought a new BMW on a whim that I couldn't really afford, and I got a new tattoo on my shoulder that was supposed to be Chinese symbols that meant freedom and prosperity (in reality it looks like I chose symbols from two different languages and I don't really know what they say!). I was ready to build a new life. I started to see that there might actually be a way out of it, but it would come with a price.

Aside from the mental and spiritual anguish of having to un-think a certain way, one of the most damaging practices of Scientology is something called disconnection. It is a shunning process where members are told they must cease all contact with people who are antagonistic against Scientology, even if what those people are saying is true, and even if they are your closest family members or friends. I was naive to think that somehow that wouldn't happen to me, but the control mechanism placed on members was swift in its Pavlovian response.

When it was officially announced that I was declared what they call a "Suppressive Person," (SP, for short) the little minions went about their business trying to protect the group from my ability to stand up for myself and get information about Scientology from outside sources.

Within just a few days, roughly 90 percent of my friends and associates disconnected from me. Word spread through phone calls and faxes from Scientology officials and people on Facebook sending private messages to each other. I couldn't believe it. Some of my closest friends, including many of whom I would have done anything for, suddenly refused contact with me out of fear and manipulation. I was in complete shock.

Most of the next few months were spent primarily in isolation, learning as much as I could about everything about Scientology that was previously hidden from me. The few bright spots included any time spent with my daughter and trying to make new friends out of others who were going through some type of similar situation. There was so much that I still couldn't reconcile in my own mind and I was having a hard time.

My daughter, Ella, and her mother moved back to Clearwater, FL, which is considered the Scientology "Mecca", and I moved back to Georgia in January of 2012. We had an arrangement where I would see Ella regularly every few weeks, and I was determined to never let that change. I still had a house in Georgia that I was renting out because it lost too much value to sell in the housing market crash, and luckily the renters vacated and I could move back in. Plus, my parents and my brother and his family all lived nearby as well.

Then, right after getting settled in, I got a letter from an attorney representing the Scientologists I sold my business to. I had websites that were used to get people interested in Narconon centers, and earned quite a bit from those sites. Since I no longer wanted anything to do with Narconon, I decided to sell them and agreed to a two-year payment plan. Just over a year into it, they capitalized on a loophole in our contract and walked away with the bulk of the business for only about half of what they owed me. I had failed to get an attorney to draft a sellers agreement or to approve the one that the buyers presented to me, and I didn't spot the liability in the contract the way it was written.

I was devastated all over again. I was going to use the more than $150,000 they still owed to rebuild a new life, and now that was gone, too. To say it was like pouring salt on a wound was a major understatement. I was crushed. I was hurt and angry and ready to lash out. I became the hornets' nest that got kicked one too many times, and I was ready for some revenge.

I feel like I must add this disclaimer here - I fully respect anyone's personal beliefs, even those people still involved in Scientology. Who am I to tell someone which gods they should worship, which creation theory they like best, what prayers they should say or rituals they should follow? But where I have to take a stand is when those beliefs are put into practices that are harming other people or somehow infringing upon their rights. There is a big difference. Scientology is only a more recent example of people being harmed in the name of religion.

What has transpired since my exit and its initial trauma was recently defined for me in something I read called *The Book of Forgiving*, by Desmond Tutu and his daughter, Mpho Tutu. In it, they provide a Fourfold Path to Forgiveness, which is Telling the Story, Naming the Hurt, Granting Forgiveness and then Renewing or Releasing the

Relationship. What they describe in the book is what I've been going through for many years now, and I've had to learn some very difficult and also rewarding lessons on this journey.

Archbishop Desmond Tutu is famous for his work in South Africa and the Truth and Reconciliation Commission after the fall of the apartheid government, and won the Nobel Peace Prize in 1984. One of the central messages in *The Book of Forgiving* talks about either being stuck in the never ending cycle of retaliation after someone has been hurt, or eventually deciding to forgive and be able to transcend peace. This has been one of the many references that has helped me tremendously in recent times. Writing this book has been a continuation of that process.

2. DOWN, BUT NOT OUT

I spent almost an entire year of my life trying to make sense of what was happening and how I had gotten to that point. I ached in ways I didn't even know were possible. I felt like my soul was ripped open and its tenderness exposed to the elements, like a root canal for the heart without anesthetic. For a while I was pretty much just going through motions in life at times. Sure, I had some good days, as thankfully there was still a tiny flicker or spark inside, and that was enough to keep me going. Most days I wrestled with an attempt to balance out the hurt part of me wanting to be a victim and the motivational part of me wanting to own my responsibility in the situation, dust myself off, and move on. To this day I believe that somewhere in between there is a happy medium, but I do know that eventually I had to stop feeling sorry for myself and figure out how I was going to fix it and move forward in life.

One of the more difficult things about reintegrating into the real world after being wrapped up in the insulated group I had been a part of for so long, was trying to lose parts of that identity that still hung around. They have their own lingo that they use frequently, and consciously not using those words and phrases definitely took some effort. As I continued to emerge from that fog, I had decided to step out from another part of my old identity. Back when I worked with Narconon I felt like I always had to make my story worse than it was when it came to my previous underage alcohol use. In reality, I was a directionless kid who needed to find some purposeful work that was fulfilling and a group of people who were socially supportive. I felt like I had reached a maturity level that I could now drink alcohol moderately and responsibly. This echoed research from the National Epidemiologic Survey on Alcohol and Related Conditions (NESARC) mentioned by two experts I interviewed for a documentary I produced a year or so prior. Many people simply grow out of their previous patterns of behavior with a change in understanding, environment or behavior.

My dad was managing a couple artists out of Nashville at the time named Adam Craig and Chris Weaver. I had spent a lot of time on the road and logged a lot of miles listening to their music. A few songs from the Chris Weaver Band were timely for me and I'll always be thankful for his music helping me through some of those tough times. I enjoyed going to some of their shows as well, as live music creates a connection on an even deeper level for me, just as it does for a lot of other people.

One day Chris was in Georgia and I met up with him and his date for dinner. I was appreciative that he had invited me, and I was starting to feel a bit more upbeat. That day I decided I was going to have a drink with him, so I ordered a beer. I told him and his date that it had been 12 years since my last drink, and their response was just what I needed at that time, neither judging me for having one nor for having gone so long without one. After that first one, I had one more. And that was it. We finished our dinner and I said goodbye. On the way home I was proud of myself, not only for proving that I was in control over my actions and behavior, but also that I was able to shed one more piece of my old skin. It was one of many changes that were to come, and I'm not saying others should do the same, but it was something that seemed okay for me.

As I gained a bit more confidence, I also decided that I really needed to quit smoking cigarettes. It had been almost 17 years, and another part of the old me I wanted to let go. I had quit one time for a few months prior to that, but didn't really want to, so it didn't last. I had always told myself that when I truly felt like it was having a real impact on my health that I would quit. Shortly after I moved back to Georgia from Oklahoma I had gotten a pretty severe cold and really felt like shit. I noticed that my cough was lingering longer and that I could feel it in my chest more than usual. I thought about it for a day or so, and realized I had to be honest with myself and that I really needed to quit. Besides, if I was going to start dating again, I would have a much better chance at finding someone if I wasn't automatically ruled out by those seeking non-smokers.

I used to joke that I was a "conscious smoker," in that I tried to cover up the smell as much as possible by smoking outside, religiously washing hands, always chewing on gum or mints, and staying away from people to reduce second-hand smoke. I didn't want to be offensive to others. I would also pass up cigarettes without coffee or some other suitable drink and not smoke other brands that I didn't like just to get the hit. As if any of that really mattered, but was some of the story I built around it to make myself feel better about it.

That night I looked at the pack of cigarettes that I had left. I had to laugh at myself for the reasoning behind my chosen brand. Winston promoted themselves as being 100% tobacco, compared to some chemicals found in other cigarettes, and I thought that somehow this actually made them "healthier". For a second I thought, *damnit, I only have three left, maybe I should buy one more pack and wean off them slowly*, but then had to laugh at myself again. So there it was, I had to face the reality of only having three more cigarettes, and that the next day would by my last day as a smoker.

One of my favorite things was to pair coffee

and cigarettes together. There were many days that I just couldn't have one without the other. So that morning, I poured my first cup of coffee and stepped outside to have a smoke. I wanted to savor it. The feel of the lighter in my hand, and the flick of the wheel to spark the flame. Immediately after the first draw and exhale the familiar tiny buzz followed by a sense of calm. Man, that was nice.

And then I got back inside and tried to take a deep breath. I couldn't. I coughed uncontrollably and my throat and chest burned. It wasn't worth it. I realized that if I wanted to quit I had to make it less enjoyable, so I decided that my last two cigarettes would have to be without coffee.

A bit later that day I stepped out and had another smoke. This one was considerably less enjoyable, but my nicotine craving demanded that I have that cigarette. Afterward I paid close attention to how badly my mouth tasted and my hands smelled, reinforcing the decision to stop.

Finally, a couple hours later it was time for my last smoke. I really made this process a big deal mentally, like walking out the door with full intention that it would be my last time. I looked down at my hands, holding the cigarette and seeing how foreign it now appeared to me, and that act of lighting it suddenly took much more effort. The tobacco no longer smelled sweet and the filter was nearly gagging me. As I smoked, I observed how my nostrils, mouth and throat felt and how much worse smoking made me feel on top of being sick. That solidified it.

It finally crossed over for me mentally to be not worth the nicotine hit, and I was absolutely sure that I was done. I took one last drag to seal the deal.

Over the next few days I definitely experienced some heavy cravings. I would usually get through them by filling that time with something else, such as a phone call, some short exercises or some other task. One of my favorites turned out to be simply sitting there and taking a few deep breaths and being grateful for my choice to be healthier and envisioning my new life without smoking. Usually those intense cravings would only last a few minutes or so, and then after about a week they were barely present at all. Eventually they were completely gone.

One thing I noticed about nicotine withdrawal is that the same thing that I would crave in order to calm me down was actually the thing that made situations more tense. In other words, much of the stress and anxiety that I would feel during everyday situations were amplified by the nicotine craving, even though I really thought for a long time that smoking was helping to relieve stress. As time went on after quitting, I became even more calm and relaxed than I was before and found it easier to be present.

That was March of 2012, and that same month I signed up for the online dating site Match.com. Even though I still felt broken and emotionally drained at times, it had been a year since I had even been out on a date and thought I would give it a try. I had spent a whole year trying to just not be an emotional wreck. It is difficult to convey the emptiness and loneliness that I felt for so long. I would sit for hours and hours at my computer in the dark with very little interaction with others. When I would go on road trips I would sometimes drive hundreds of miles in silence when I was numb, and other times I would play music as loud as possible when I wanted to feel some emotion. Much of it I had to go through on my own, and I definitely could have benefited from the help of a good therapist, on many levels. But here I was, after a long period of reckoning, ready to re-enter the world socially, and romantically, or at least take a step in that direction.

I figured I didn't want to play any games and would be really open and honest about my past, because if someone knew all the shit about that and wasn't scared away, then it was worth the effort. I'm sure I sounded pretty crazy talking about Scientology, and I think some of the women were interested in the conversation as more like bizarre entertainment than any actual interest in a romantic relationship. Most of them just wanted to know if I had ever met Tom Cruise, of course (which I had, and wasn't impressed).

Although I had some dates and many phone conversations, I still wasn't finding someone I really connected with on enough levels. Along the way I had gotten a message on Facebook from a girl I had gone to high school with named Hayley. She told me that she saw my profile on Match and that she thought I would hit it off with her boss, Leslie. She gave me Leslie's email and phone number. I thanked her and said I would email her, but it took me a few weeks to actually do so.

Then, after a couple emails and a great phone conversation or two, Leslie and I set up our first date in June. She suggested a place called Elevation Chop House in Kennesaw, which was a cool restaurant on the second floor of a building at a local airport. I arrived first, and waited out front for her. Even though it was only a few minutes, it seemed like an eternity. I was so nervous, almost like I knew this first date was more important than all the others. Then, she walked round the corner, and I was in awe of this confident, tall blonde wearing lime green pants and high heels walking toward me. Oh shit. I was suddenly even more nervous and now had nowhere to hide.

"Luke?" she sort of stated and asked at the same time. "Yeah, hi!" I replied as she moved in for a quick hug and I tried to hide my sweaty palms and armpits.

We went up the stairs to a nice table overlooking the runway and just hit it off right away. She was as present and interested as I felt I was, and we both sort of laid it all out on the table, not holding anything back. We both had gotten divorced about the same time, although she didn't have any children yet. It was amazing and so refreshing to be able to talk about things so freely. I didn't feel like I was being judged, and gradually become more comfortable in her presence. The night carried on, and we went to a nearby pizza place called Mellow Mushroom so we could keep talking. We sat on the patio and she ordered an Abita Purple Haze. I found it cool that this intelligent, confident, classy woman was totally comfortable ordering a beer on a first date, and she seemed to know more about football than I did. Even though it was pretty obvious to me that she was out of my league, it still felt so natural to be there.

It was a weeknight, so the restaurant closed early, and I was bummed because even though we had been talking for hours by then, it really felt like the conversation was just getting started, because it was. It went so well that we set another date for later that week.

I couldn't wait for that day to come. This time we met at Pure Tacqueria in Woodstock. As we caught up on the last few days and ate some chips and salsa, the loud music sort of made the conversation a little awkward at times because it was hard to hear. However, I was gaining a bit of confidence and said, "I'd love to hire you away from your company to work with me some day at Catton Communications."

I was really naive and had no idea how much money she made at her current job and didn't really have much of a company to speak of, yet. Also the fact that she graduated from the University of Virginia, which is a school that I could never have gotten into, and that I never even completed a full year of college, again confirmed that I had no idea what I was really talking about.

With a look of surprise on her face, she asked, "what do you mean by 'communications'"?

I froze and suddenly felt like there was more attention on me than there should be, and I wasn't sure how to answer that question in a way that might be impressive to her, let alone sound anywhere close to intelligent. I went from confident to instantly self conscious and began to sweat. Like really sweat. The music got louder and thumped in my chest, and my heart started to race. I watched her eyes follow a bead of sweat that was rolling down my forehead. *Oh shit*, I thought, *now what?* I tried to stumble through an explanation, as each second of hesitation felt like an eternity.

"A few different things, actually," doing my best to sound like I knew what I was talking about, "such as public relations, copywriting, web development and other things."

She nodded her head indicating I had answered her question satisfactorily, or at least pretending it to be so, and then we went on to another topic. *Whew.* I think she really just felt bad for me because she could see that I was uncomfortable.

After dinner we walked around a bit and found a seat at a nice place called the Century House with some outside tables. We were pretty much alone outside, and this oddly adorable baby possum peeked out from under the porch, then darted back under after it spotted us. Once again we kept talking until the restaurant closed (which continued to be a theme for us), and we had to wrap it up.

As I walked her back to her car, I started to get really nervous, because it seemed like a kiss was imminent. Here I was, in my mid-thirties, feeling like a teenager again. Only this time the awkwardness quickly disappeared when the moment arrived, as it seemed so familiar and comfortable, like we were meant to be there together.

Over the next few months we spent as much time together as we possibly could. I had found someone who was very intelligent, successful, loving, empathetic and beautiful and I had managed, for a while at least, to not chase her off.

Despite Leslie's complete acceptance of me, I still had a very difficult time with intimacy at first. I didn't feel like I deserved love and still wasn't sure if I could love someone enough in return since I felt so flawed and damaged. I felt inadequate in so many ways as I struggled to be comfortable, and I was ashamed of not being able to be fully present with her, yet she was patient and encouraging. Still, I continued to beat myself up and say that she deserved more, my pattern of self-abnegation. She saw through it all, though, and was even gracious, after getting out of an abusive relationship following her divorce. She knew that at the very least I wasn't a threat to her.

In addition to the already difficult things that most divorced people go through, I had all the Scientology bullshit that I was still trying to shed.

People like to use the peeling the layers of an onion analogy for a lot of things. To me, this was more like pulling shrapnel or buckshot out that had been deeply embedded, with scar tissue over it, then waiting for it to heal again without a bandage. The process was very difficult for me, because I still carried around so much shame and guilt over all that I had been through and taken part in, and I still felt like a failure in many ways. Looking back, I was also acting in a selfish way as a result, because I had overlooked anything that she may have been through prior to our relationship as well.

As a result, we wound up spending some time apart because I wasn't sure what I wanted, and she wasn't going to necessarily wait around for me to decide. I had pushed her away, and the time apart was very difficult for both of us. I remember bawling hysterically one night because I just couldn't understand why I messed that up, and how miserable I was with the thought of having screwed it all up. I felt a new loss, and it was intense on top of old wounds, and this one was more easily identifiable for me as being self-inflicted.

I've come to accept that pain and loss are inevitable forms of suffering. They are things we all must experience, but too often the attempt to try our damnedest to avoid these by running away from them or pretending they're not there only makes the situations worse. The resistance means that which is unavoidable continues to hover like a dark cloud. For me at that time, I was running away from love and intimacy because I still felt I didn't deserve it. I eventually realized that this self-pity and mental flagellation had to stop. In order to heal, I had to accept myself and what I had done in order to allow positive thoughts, feelings, relationships and experiences.

Being afraid of getting hurt or hurting another again was preventing me from healing and from loving and being loved. The fear of potential pain is often worse than the actual experience of pain or discomfort. I think that's a recurring theme for a lot of people, though. As Master Oogway humbly said in the children's move *Kung Fu Panda*, "One often meets his destiny on the road he takes to avoid it." Double the effort and more pain and worry, when standing in there to face it would be easier to begin with.

Much like building muscle mass from working out, we also grow when we tear. Just as the tissue reconnects and expands to become stronger, so does our spirit. The soreness is a brief reminder of what we have endured, and also *that we can endure*, and I was trying to trust that no matter what happened in the future, I would ultimately be okay.

Sometimes these tears are so tiny that we barely notice, while other times we feel completely broken. Throughout life these tears may help accumulate understanding, and when we break we often come out on the other side completely changed. This definitely happened for me then, and even several times since then in different areas. I've also developed more of an understanding since then of how our experiences are filtered through our thoughts, beliefs and perceptions, and we can choose to see things differently and create meaning in our lives. The same exact thing can happen to two different people, yet they have totally different experiences and results. Whether it turns out positive or remains negative in the end is up to them.

Another invaluable aspect of breaking open is that we become more vulnerable. Our tenderness is exposed when the hard shell is no longer covering it. This vulnerability is an invitation for connection with others. It is also where real, heartfelt communication can reside. As I looked deeper, this is what I was really experiencing with Leslie, and it was a mutual vulnerability that I had taken for granted. She was opening up to me as well, and I hadn't noticed just how much she was also risking emotionally to do so. I had leaned on her a lot in the beginning.

After a few weeks apart I began emailing, calling and texting her periodically. I asked to see her again. She would make excuses as to why she couldn't, as I later found out that she was really just watching *Blue Planet* or something on The Food Network. She eventually agreed, reluctantly, despite her own fears of getting hurt again. Thankfully, something spoke to her that there was more of a connection that either of us could ignore, and we finally arranged a time to meet.

After a few months of not seeing each other, we met up at one of our old favorite places -

Marlow's in Kennesaw. I got there first and anxiously waited for her arrival. She came in and sat down next to me, after a somewhat hesitant hug, and had a bit of a skeptical look on her face. What started off as a slow apology from me eventually became a much more relaxed conversation. It was familiar again. I was grateful. We both missed each other, deeply, and there was no denying it. We really were in love, and I promised her that I wasn't going to flake like that again and that I really wanted to be with her.

After that night, we were committed to seeing where things went together. At the end of the year I introduced Ella to Leslie, which was a huge deal for me. I had promised myself I would only let Ella develop a relationship with a woman that I really loved. It wasn't long before Ella was asking me if Leslie was going to be her step mother and if she was going to get to be a big sister. She was also excited because she loved Leslie's pugs, June (Carter Cash) and Otis (Redding).

Leslie moved in with me at the end of July in 2013, and we began looking for a home together. We quickly found a house in Kennesaw that we loved, and put in an offer. I could see the kids playing in the backyard already, and I was hopeful. Once our offer was accepted, we listed my house in Canton for sale. We were so excited, and I could really start to feel this new life I had envisioned coming together, built on our growing love.

One evening after I had been traveling with

Ella to bring her back to Florida, I got home and Leslie was sitting at the kitchen table. We were catching up on how the day went. She had a look on her face that I wasn't sure about and hadn't really seen before. I asked her if there was anything else, and she said no and that she was going to go to bed. I told her I was going to check emails and read a bit and then would be up in a while.

Just a minute or so after I sat down at my desk, she appeared in the doorway.

"Well, there was one more thing," she said, with that indescribable look still on her face. I got up and joined her in the hallway. She grabbed my hands and looked up at me, as if not knowing what to expect, and then exclaimed, "I'm pregnant." I froze for a second and looked at her to double-check if she was serious. Her eyes confirmed it with a look of uncertainty about the future. My initial reaction was to laugh and cry at the same time at how beautiful it was and how happy I felt. Tears welled up in my eyes as I held her and looked down.

"Really?! That is wonderful! I love you!"

We both cried and hugged and wiped tears away. During that moment, there wasn't a separate her and me, it was a unified us. She confessed that she had known since the day before and wasn't sure how I was going to respond. She was relieved that I was happy, and said that it helped ease some of her fears. We were on our way to starting a family, and I returned to the vision in my mind of the kids playing in the backyard together at our new house, which already had a play set. It was real hope at a good life, something that had escaped me for what seemed like an eternity.

In the last several years I have learned to look for signs from the Universe, and that week a huge sign about how we were supposed to be in each others' lives at that time came in three forms. First we found out we were having a baby, then we closed on the new house, and to finish it up, we accepted an offer on my house that was for the exact amount I was hoping for. It couldn't have been a more perfect transition into the next phase of life.

That November we hosted our combined families for Thanksgiving at our new home. We had just gotten our latest ultrasound, and had a gender confirmation ultrasound done as well at 14 weeks, and both said we were having a girl. We had ordered gender reveal cupcakes for the occasion, and everyone was so happy to see and hear the news.

A few weeks later, Leslie and I were sitting in the waiting room at her doctor's office getting ready for the 20 week anatomy ultrasound. We were nervous and excited, and I made a joke about how many times people find out the baby is a different gender than what they thought. I said, "wouldn't it be funny if that happened to us?!"

When it was our turn, the ultrasound technician went about taking all the measurements and confirmed the baby was healthy and growing on schedule. It was so amazing to watch the beating heart up on the screen, and the tiny little hands and feet.

"Do you want to know the gender?" asked the technician.

"Oh, we already know we're having a girl," we replied, in unison.

But then, a pause.

"Umm, see this part right here?" she said as she pointed to the screen. "This is a boy!"

We didn't know if she was kidding at first, but she wrote "boy" up on the screen and our jaws hit the floor. Shock led to laughter to tears to a bit of confusion. We were already well on the way to thinking we were having a girl, and now that suddenly changed. We went out and immediately called our parents when we got into the car and shared the news. It took a bit to adjust, but soon we were well into the baby boy mindset. Our son Rhett was born on May 26, 2014, which also happened to be Memorial Day that year.

3. TAKING A STAND

During the summer of 2012 there were some news stories coming out about several deaths involving patients at Narconon centers, specifically in Georgia and Oklahoma. I decided that I could lend a hand to the victims' families by speaking out about what I knew about the organization and its ties to Scientology. I started contributing to some forums and websites and doing some interviews. It was also as a form of retribution for their actions against me and others, as well as a way to help make up for the time that I had worked for them. This eventually led to my writing the book.

The interviews grew as the news got bigger, which started to include larger publications and network affiliate television stations. There was a string of three fatalities in Oklahoma alone within a period of nine months. Overall, there wound up being four deaths tied to Narconon Arrowhead, as well as a crippling overdose, and one death tied to the Georgia facility, and all of the families had filed civil lawsuits. I started helping attorneys who were representing the victims' families, and also being interviewed by criminal investigators in both states.

One interview in Georgia was with WSB-TV, Atlanta's ABC affiliate. I had been put in touch with the law firm representing the family and was helping them decode some of the Scientology language they found in various discovery documents, acting as sort of an interpreter and educator for attorney Jeff Harris and his team as well as the media outlets covering the case. For example, the reporter, Jodie Fleischer, referenced a document that the head of Narconon Georgia wrote directly to church of Scientology officials. I was asked if it was common for Narconon officials to report directly to Scientology officials, and I confirmed that it was definitely a normal part of their operations. Despite their denials, here was at least one piece of clear evidence of that fact. In addition to coverage by Jodie Fleischer for WSB TV, there was also coordinated coverage with Christian Boone from the *Atlanta Journal & Constitution* and Pete Combs from WSB Radio.

The interview was at the law firm's office in Atlanta, and also present were the sister and mother of the young man, Patrick Desmond, who died in the hospital after an overdose that occurred while hanging out with employees of the facility one night. When I was introduced to them, I felt ashamed that I had once promoted the program, and when they thanked me for speaking out it suddenly became very real to me that this was way bigger than my personal redemption. There was much more at stake to both hold people accountable for their actions but also to make amends for what I was involved with for so long, whether knowingly or unknowingly. Now it wasn't just about trying to show them they shouldn't have messed with me, but so much more, like helping families start to heal as well. I felt a deep sadness for their loss, which motivated me even more to try and help seek justice.

That case went on to settle out of court on a Friday afternoon before jury selection was to begin the following Monday. I remember being happy for Patrick's family that they received a settlement and also relieved that I didn't have to testify, but also disappointed that all of the information found during the discovery period wouldn't get to be presented in a trial. Thankfully, much of it was not sealed as it was filed during various pretrial motions, as well as a damning ruling from the judge. DeKalb County State Court Judge Stacey Hydrick issued sanctions against Narconon of Georgia, stating that the program's director, Mary Rieser, lied under oath and hid evidence. One piece of evidence was the previous document I mentioned, which was found by Narconon's own attorneys and sent over to the Plaintiff's attorneys.

Several months later I was brought into criminal investigations in three states by three to what was being communicated. It must not have been too bad, because it made the final cut.

Before I knew it, the interviews were over, and I had to leave to head back to the airport to catch my flight home to Atlanta. With the car waiting out front, I said goodbye to Anna, Harry and the production staff and they got one more b-roll shot of Eric and me walking, and then I was whisked away back to JFK. I wound up barely making it through security and to the gate in time to board, sweating through my dress shirt. It was a smaller regional jet, so we boarded quickly and pulled away from the gate in what seemed like just a few minutes, and were soon in the air heading back to Georgia. I finally caught my breath a bit and it started to sink in what had just happened. I remember looking out the window of the plane and saw Arthur Ashe tennis stadium, where the U.S. Open is held, and thought of Leslie, who had been a state champion tennis player in high school.

It had been cold and windy in NYC, but it was warm and sunny in Atlanta when I landed late that Friday afternoon. I was in a great mood, so much so that I didn't even care that traffic was terrible. I just opened my sunroof and played music and enjoyed the feeling of accomplishment. I was thinking back to watching the first Rock Center segment about Narconon and remember saying to myself that I should be on that show with all that I knew. Here it was just a few months later and it had actually happened. I had gone from a silent victim to a national whistleblower. A few days later NBC sent a camera man to my house to grab some more b-roll footage of me working at a computer to use in the final editing.

The episode was eventually scheduled to air on Friday, April 5th, 2013. I had stayed home to watch it and respond to messages on Tony Ortega's site, on Facebook and via phone calls and texts. Anticipation had built all day. I've had my share of disappointments, and Scientology had a history of getting shows pulled due to legal threats, so I wasn't going to count on anything until it was done. My heart was pounding as it came on. I got a call just before it from my dad, who was on the road with Adam Craig and his band, and they were all watching from the hotel before their performance. During the show it was terrifying and fun and exciting to interact with people who were watching it and communicating about it. At the same time I felt incredibly exposed and lonely. Nonetheless, when the show was over I was very proud and relieved that it had finally aired.

I felt that between that show airing, the book and the work with the attorneys, I had started to make enough public impact, even though my involvement would be sporadic over time afterward. I had to feel okay with my level of contribution toward justice and helping to right many of the wrongs I had previously supported.

I eventually pulled the book from publication several months later. While I was criticized by some people for doing so, with online speculation that I had somehow caved or cut a deal with Scientology, it really had nothing to do with that at all. In fact, I remained involved in working with attorneys and investigators on helping with the legal retributions, I just didn't keep posting about it or make my actions broadly known. The book, for me, was very personal, and I felt I had communicated what I needed to. My life was changing in such a positive way that I didn't want to keep fighting publicly, and I also turned down all future media requests for various interviews, shows and productions. I just didn't want that to be a defining part of my identity anymore. Maybe someday I'll release a revised version of it for some of the historical information it contained.

In June of 2014, I received a subpoena to testify before a criminal investigation into Narconon Arrowhead by the Oklahoma Attorney General's office. They had sent it to a multicounty grand jury to review some of the evidence that the state had gathered up to that point. Once the dates were worked out, the Oklahoma AG's office booked a flight and hotel for me to testify at the end of the month. On the day of travel, I had a layover at Dallas-Ft. Worth Airport, but my connecting flight got cancelled, and I was bumped to the next morning. Rather than waiting for the flight and potentially being late, I was able to get a rental car and drove from Dallas up to Oklahoma City. It was a very odd and lonely feeling crossing that Oklahoma border just before sunset that summer night. It had been two and a half years since I left Oklahoma, and I certainly hadn't envisioned returning for that purpose. On one hand I was sad for all of the people and circumstances involved, while on the other I was glad to do my share to keep telling the truth of what I knew and had experienced to those with the capacity to take action.

I wound up getting to the hotel fairly late that evening, and I was paranoid that there were potentially private investigators trying to keep an eye on me while I was there. Every time I saw someone who might have looked my way, I stopped to observe them for a bit to see if they really were watching me. I didn't wind up seeing anything out of the ordinary, and thankfully I slept much better that evening than I had when traveling to New York the previous year. Although Scientology has admittedly used private investigators to follow people for decades, and still do so today to harass whistleblowers and intimidate witnesses, I never found any evidence that they had dispatched one my direction, thankfully.

The next morning, when I arrived at the Attorney General's office, I was put in a room to wait with Eric Tenorio. It was great seeing him again, and it was also weird to put that in context with the first time I met him back in 1998 at Narconon there in Oklahoma, and how the last time I saw him was in New York filming an interview for national television. It would have been easy to go down a

different agencies. First I was contacted by agents Kevin Kearney and Matt Entrekin with the Georgia Insurance Commissioner's fraud department and also Paul Wilkening from the Oklahoma Insurance Commissioner's fraud department. They traveled to meet me at a Hampton Inn conference room in Canton and asked a lot of questions about how Narconon operated and what the relationship was to the church of Scientology. The delegation from Oklahoma asked where the records might be kept at the facility and requested a diagram of the property with labels in case they were going to perform a raid similar to one that was done at the Georgia facility. I brought a voice recorder with me since I was alone, and put it on the table. Paul Wilkening said, "oh good, we should record this too," and his partner set his phone on the table and pressed record as well.

This meeting was eventually followed by a another one at the Georgia Insurance Commissioner's office in Atlanta, where the lead investigator, Sherry Mowell, asked questions about evidence they had found. I recorded that meeting as well, openly placing my voice recorder on the table for my protection. However, after much deliberation about what they were going to do with the evidence they had, they ultimately declined to file charges because there had to be a specific person named. Although they indicated there was evidence of fraud, they couldn't nail down who were the individuals responsible for it, as Mary Rieser and the other employees pointed fingers at each other and even

tried to blame their billing company. During this time, the program requested to enter into a non-prosecutorial agreement with the Gwinnett County District Attorney, Danny Porter, where Narconon agreed to close its Georgia location for a minimum of two years and not admit any wrongdoing. Although there were people upset that two years was not enough punishment, they have not tried to open another program in the state since then.

One thing I really learned throughout this whole process, is that there is a reason for the saying that the wheels of justice turn slowly. As I look back at when specific events took place, I see that what now seems like months between some activities was actually years, and a lot happened in between. I'm apparently only recapping the highlights.

I had started to write my book at the end of 2012 and the beginning of 2013. I released it in February of 2013. Coinciding with that was another civil lawsuit sparked between Narconon and the National Association of Forensic Counselors, for fraudulently obtaining and using counselor certifications, which I had written about and a few other former staff members exposed, including one named Eric Tenorio, whom I knew well and had worked with in Oklahoma. This prompted a producer from the NBC show *Rock Center* to use as a follow-up story to one they had previously done about the deaths in Oklahoma. The producer was Anna Schecter, and NBC made arrangements for Eric and me to travel to New York City to record

interviews. I was really excited and felt like I could make a big impact through a national audience, and at the same time I was terrified of the whole event and what the outcome might be. Nonetheless, I kept moving forward. Leslie bought me two new shirts for the trip, which I still wear often, as I feel they're good luck shirts.

So, I flew up to NYC. NBC booked us to stay at the Dream hotel downtown. I got there a bit earlier than Eric, and wound up meeting up with another ex-Scientologist named Aaron to have coffee. He had also done some work with Narconon, but thankfully hadn't gotten as deeply involved nor for as long. It was great to see him and to know that there were actually many others like him who just stopped participating. After coffee I walked back to the hotel and met up with Eric, whom I hadn't seen Eric in years, and we were joined by Anna and her assistant. I was pretty uncomfortable in the swanky, modern place, and it seemed pretty surreal that I was there. It was great to see Eric again, and we wound up doing some b-roll filming right away that evening by the water before dark. Later, after Anna and her assistant left, Eric and I had dinner at the hotel and invited journalist Tony Ortega to join us. We were really excited about the upcoming show, and enjoyed a nice meal on the network's dime.

That night I couldn't sleep. I was really nervous and the room was uncomfortably modern, and I wasn't used to all the noise. Although I had

been to New York City one other time, I had never spent the night there before, and to top it off, the night club in the basement of the hotel was thumping with music that I could still hear several floors up. I just lay there hoping to fall asleep, but was afraid that I would oversleep since I was so tired. I had set my phone alarm, plus asked for a wake-up call from the front desk, but was still uncertain it would be enough. By the time I finally drifted off it felt like only a few minutes later the sun was up and my alarm was going off. I got myself ready and met Eric down in the lobby, where a car was supposed to be picking us up out front.

After some initial confusion from the driver on where he was supposed to take us, we eventually arrived at an off-site location used for filming, and the crew was already set up. Our interviewer was Harry Smith, a broadcast veteran, and he was all business, including voicing his very noticeable displeasure with the background noises. The intensity kept building inside me and it still hadn't really hit me that this was happening. After an assistant was able to get some nearby construction work to halt long enough to film, we were off.

There was really no way to fully prepare for the interview, as we didn't know exactly what they were going to ask about nor how it would be worded. I guess they wanted the natural reactions, and at one point I panicked a bit, because I stumbled over the phrase "vulnerable people," but I kept rolling and hoped my reaction wasn't too much of a distraction

long road in my mind of wondering how it all came to this and shaming myself for getting so involved, but I tried to stay focused. It helped that the Assistant Attorney General, George Burnett, kept us busy prior to our individual testimony appearances. Multicounty grand juries are called to hear evidence from many witnesses for a number of different investigations, so this was just one of the topics they were having to weigh during their convening. Before we knew it, each of us had our turn to testify, and then we were finished by lunch.

Attorney Gary Richardson, who was representing many of the Plaintiffs against Narconon in Oklahoma, had known we were in town and asked to take us to lunch. We followed him to a restaurant, and were joined by Robert Murphy, the father of Stacy Murphy, who had died of a drug overdose at Narconon's facility in Oklahoma in July of 2012. It was a full two years after her passing that there finally appeared to be some movement on criminal prosecution, though no definitive action from the State Department of Mental Health.

Once again, I was humbled by the presence of a parent who lost their child. Stacy's death was the last one that occurred at the facility, and perhaps got the most media attention. Both Gary Richardson and Robert Murphy thanked us for standing up and speaking out, and for being willing to cooperate with the criminal investigations. To my knowledge, all of Gary Richardson's clients were eventually able to settle out of court without having to go to trial.

As we finished up lunch and said goodbye, I drove Eric to the airport and dropped off the rental car. My flight didn't leave for a few hours, but I was so ready to get home. Things were already very different for me, as much had changed in my life since this evolution began. I didn't feel like I needed to or wanted to fight anymore, and that there was enough momentum to continue carrying forth justice, in whatever form that would be. It wound up being the last time I saw Eric in person as well, as we haven't crossed paths since then.

I remember feeling confident that there would finally be some criminal charges or indictments at some point against Narconon. Then news hit in August that the Oklahoma Grand Jury ran out of time before they could go through all the evidence for an indictment, and they officially recommended further investigation. A couple months later I got a call from Stephen Colburn, the new investigator at the Insurance Commissioner's office that had been handed the case. However, after about a year of digging into things more, including multiple trips to the facility and interviews with staff and others, he told me he had completed his investigation and turned it and his recommendations into his superiors.

In October of 2014 I received a call from another investigator. This time it was an FBI agent named Kurt Schichtel out of Michigan who was looking into insurance fraud allegations against Narconon and related organizations up there. He was loosely working with state agencies in Oklahoma and Georgia, but told me he didn't have jurisdiction outside of Michigan at that time in order to take on a larger racketeering investigation. He was much more tight-lipped about the specifics of what he was doing compared to the guys who worked for state agencies. After that initial conversation, there was a follow-up done in early 2015 as well, but then no more word or contact from him. I don't know what happened with it, as I never received an official subpoena and there wasn't any news coverage of criminal prosecution up there. However, there were other civil lawsuits filed by Plaintiffs in Michigan represented by Attorney Jeffrey Ray. I never spoke with him, but I did have a couple conversations with his paralegal at the time, Catherine Villanueva.

As I thought activity was winding down in November of 2015, I got another subpoena to give a deposition as a non-party witness for several civil lawsuits between Narconon and multiple Plaintiffs. However, this time it was Narconon's attorneys who issued it and wanted me to turn over communications I'd had regarding their cases. I reached out to several law firms for the Plaintiffs and none were quick to help or offer advice, which was a clear indication to me that I was on my own, so I showed up alone ready to face whatever was thrown at me.

On December 8th, I drove down to the rented office space in a high rise in Midtown Atlanta, where I met Julio Vergara, the attorney for Narconon who had issued the subpoenaed. Also present were the court reporter, and Clark Carr, the President of Narconon International. On a guess that Clark might be there, I actually had texted him the day before and offered to meet for coffee. I had one conversation with him a year or so earlier when I had drafted a suggestion for Narconon to settle all cases, admit to the fraud they were committing, restructure their licenses and admit that they were in fact a faith-based organization using Scientology. I had said that that was their only real chance at surviving the onslaught of civil and criminal legal proceedings against them and for any hope turning around their PR crisis. Of course they declined to do so, and chose to keep fighting instead and denying any wrongdoing whatsoever.

After the initial awkward handshakes, I was sworn in on camera and Julio began his barrage of questions. His demeanor went from pleasant to argumentative when he realized I wasn't going to be intimidated into saying something that wasn't true or bend to his tendency to try and reword my statements to fit his needs, especially when I had personally witnessed so much over the years. He kept rephrasing things I had said in the past, with a twist of words to make it sound in his favor, and then would try to get me to agree that what he said was true. I kept having to refute his statements and stand my ground. In addition to trying to get evidence from me for discovery, it seemed like one of his primary motives was to try and discredit me as a witness. He underestimated my knowledge and experience as we went toe to toe for hours.

Back and forth we went, throughout the day. They would then take short breaks to strategize after going through the documents I was forced to provide, and then we would reconvene for another round. It wound up being a pretty traumatic event for me. It was so similar to being badgered in a Scientology confessional, especially since Clark was present and Julio was trying to get me to admit to things that weren't true. Despite being alone and feeling like I was ganged up on, I knew I had nothing to hide, so I didn't back down. It was, however, very tense and nerve wracking. I wound up clenching my teeth so hard during the day that I actually chipped a sliver off my front tooth, and to this day I'm often reminded of that harrowing event.

Ryan Hamilton, the Plaintiffs' attorney, was present on the speaker phone to listen in, but he wasn't representing me nor necessarily on my side. This was of great benefit to him, though, as he was able to get a lot of information in my deposition, at their expense.

We eventually hit a stalemate after Julio had thrown everything at me that he could. He kept the deposition open, and I never got a transcript or video of it, though Hamilton's cases were all eventually settled out of court as well to my knowledge. Sometimes I wish I could go back and view that tape, as I was proud of myself for speaking the truth and standing my ground. However, I was utterly drained after being there for a total of 9 hours, without support, and I hadn't had lunch nor dinner yet. By the time I finally got home I was a complete wreck. Not only did I have a severe headache from talking so much and barely eating, but I had an intense knot in my chest that went through to my back. At one point I even thought I might be having a heart attack. I was seriously concerned because it was an excruciating pain of constriction that I hadn't experienced before. I took some Advil and tried to relax and eat something, and then just crashed on the couch and broke down and cried in my wife's lap. I wept over not just how difficult it was and how terrible I felt, but for all of the associated pain attached to them as a whole. *Why won't they just go away?* Although I felt that it turned out well in terms of being able to communicate what was necessary, I was so depleted that my body's reaction was to weep as a way of trying to let go of all of the stored tension and angst from the day. I didn't know how much I had left to give after that.

Scientology and its affiliated organizations have gained reputations for being bullies, which is honestly putting it very mildly. Many of the documented things they have done to people are unbelievably terrible for a tax-exempt organization, and unconscionable for a church. The tactics used on me alone felt like mental and spiritual torture at times, and I still had a mild case compared to plenty of others. The act of enforced disconnection was a brutal thing to overcome, and something that I still have to deal with every day. There are many people, especially children who were raised in it, who have had it far worse than I have, though. Stories of parents and grandparents refusing to see their children or grandchildren, of siblings never talking to each other again, and of adult children disconnecting from their parents. In some cases, people died before they ever had a chance to repair their relationships that were broken apart by L. Ron Hubbard's sadistic treatments and rules for paranoid control. Leah Remini's show on A&E, *Scientology and the Aftermath*, helped to bring much of this to light over three seasons, as well as well as Lawrence Wright's book *Going Clear* and Alex Gibney's HBO documentary of the same name, let alone the years' worth of reporting from Tony Ortega and former Scientology official Mike Rinder's blog.

Experiencing this has created a space inside of me that is much more aware of those who suffer from bullying and mental torture than I ever realized before. And, having self-identified as an empathic introvert, some of these feelings hit pretty hard.

I feel that one of the most saddening and horrible types of tragedies that have occurred in America in recent years has been violence among children and young adults. From planned massive attacks to repetitive bullying and self-inflicted wounds, the pain and suffering felt by these young people is then acted out in other ways. There have been heart-wrenching stories throughout the country, and despite the fact that many experts have tried to find the source of these problems or use various measures to prevent them from repeating in other areas, I believe that they have largely missed the boat on finding a real solution. I believe that most of these lost souls were missing real connection in their lives that could have helped them find meaning and give them support, purpose and direction as well as a sense of belonging - those who were inflicting the harm as well as those suffering directly from it who decided to act or react in unimaginable ways.

When I was 16, there was a kid named Brian Head who had been picked on for many years. From elementary school until high school I recall numerous times where he had gotten into relatively minor, but nonetheless hurtful, altercations with other kids. Some of these stuck out as being more vivid and harmful than others, such as when a kid punched him in the face and bloodied his nose when Brian told him to quit making fun of him, and another time when a kid pushed him down and then jumped off the steps onto his back, undoubtedly bruising him badly and leaving footprints on his shirt. There were also outbursts in class sometimes where he would lash out at someone who was harassing him, yet he was often the one who would get in trouble with the teachers. I have a tough time writing about this, because I feel so sorry for the pain and suffering he endured.

Apparently one day in high school he had finally had enough. He brought a gun to school, and after threatening to kill another student who was teasing him, he turned it on himself and took his own life in the classroom.

As shocking as it was back then in 1994, the magnitude of it really didn't hit me until several years ago when I was working to process my own feelings of being an outcast of sorts. I continually ran though my mind times throughout my childhood when I was a witness to him being picked on, as well as other people being picked on, and felt that I could have and should have done something differently. Had I stuck up for him, would he still be alive today? Had I shown compassion toward him back then, and encouraged others to do the same, would Brian have wound up in such pain that he wanted to end his own life? Of course I'll never know the answer to that, but it doesn't mean I can't play a part in preventing that from happening to others in the future, whether through raising a voice in opposition of bullying, or displaying compassion and showing support for individuals who are suffering.

Much of today's bullying is perpetrated online, through nasty comments and horrible statements made carelessly without any regard for the well-being of another. People are quick to fire off hurtful posts or replies without a second thought about whether they would want someone treating them or their loved ones that way, either online or in person. Social media can be a venue for people who feel inadequate in some way, picked on or left out IRL (in real life) who then turn that back on others while hiding behind a screen name and pushing buttons on their computer, tablet or phone. There is little to no regard for what happens to the person receiving those comments. Their ridicule can cause real harm though, they're not "just words." In fact, a study published in the journal *Lancet Psychiatry* in April of 2015 showed that children who were bullied were up to 60% more likely to have mental health problems as adults, compared to those who were abused in other ways.

Although I thankfully did not really experience being bullied growing up, I witnessed it with my brother occasionally. There were times when I was younger that I remember a few kids being really mean to him, and others where they would goad him because he tended to have a shorter fuse. When I was in second grade there was a kid in the neighborhood who actually forced his way into our home after school and was trying to attack my brother. Another kid named Rod, who was the older brother of my best friend back then, was bullying him one afternoon and I picked up a pinecone and stood in between them. Rod looked at me and said, "what are you going to do, throw that at me?" Then he looked back at my brother as if he were about to go after him, and so I threw that pinecone as hard as I could and nailed him right between the eyes. It was enough to stun him, and as we started to run away I saw tiny droplets of blood appear on his face in a distinct pattern. I remember being terrified of getting my own ass beat, but also proud for standing up to him. I never understood why kids could be so mean like that, and I felt so bad that my brother was hurting, more so emotionally than physically. I hated seeing him in pain, and I know that he still carries some of that pain around with him today.

I certainly got a taste of being bullied later when people were forced to disconnect from me and retaliate in different ways for standing up for my sanity. Then, when I thrust myself and my story out there for anyone to see, some of the commentary was directed at me in an attempt to attack my character and then get me to break in some sort of way.

At one point, a website was put up about me (and others who were taking a stand) and multiple message boards continued to scrutinize every aspect about the stories. One comment thread included the statement by someone that I should just go kill myself. Another person, whom I actually knew and had disconnected from me, told me that I was the worst person ever and that I should just die, literally die because the world would be better off without me. There were several others as well that cut me very deeply emotionally at the time, and I just wasn't really prepared for those kinds of messages.

Whether any of these were said lightly or not, they were definitely hurtful, especially since I was trying to do the right thing and stand up for myself and others who had been harmed. What made them worse was the fact that when I was younger I had actually contemplated suicide, as many teens or young adults do at some point in their lives when they're feeling really low or depressed. However, I eventually realized that those thoughts, along with others, can pass if I choose to recognize them for what they are and let them go. I was also able to re-examine the situation and understand that I had to be confident in myself and what I was doing and learn to listen to the overwhelming majority of people who were supportive and thankful.

Other former members who dared to speak up didn't fare so well. Some fell back into their previous self-destructive behaviors, and a few others believed the lies they were told about not being able to make it "on the outside" and reluctantly rejoined the organization out of fear of things getting worse. One troubled young man named Beau Griffis wound up falling to his death off the 7th floor of a building in State College, PA in May of 2014. His roommate at Narconon Arrowhead was Gabriel Graves, who had died at the facility. Beau attempted to be an outspoken critic, but he hadn't appeared stable to me during the brief interaction I had with him online and a single phone conversation, and I had encouraged him to get real help, even pleading with one of his friends that something wasn't right.

Few people involved back then subjected themselves to what I had been going through and the weight I felt I was personally carrying at times, both publicly and behind the scenes. At the same time I do realize that there were others who bore much heavier burdens, and still do to this day. I'm thankful that I had the support of loved ones and the majority of those who were following the story lines.

Eventually things really tapered off for a while

on the legal front as I went about rebuilding my life. Then one day in March of 2017 I got yet another subpoena from an attorney in Oklahoma named Mike Atkinson. He was representing Heather Landmeier, who had suffered irreversible damage following an overdose and had allegedly gotten drugs from a staff member at Narconon. Her case had been stalled for a long time and was finally nearing a trial. Atkinson flew out to Georgia and found a local place to take my deposition later that Spring. There were attorneys present for Narconon as well, but this time it was much more straightforward and without much argument. It was finished in about an hour or so. A few weeks later Mr. Atkinson called me and said that the case had finally settled out of court.

The pattern was similar for almost all of the cases. Narconon represented themselves to be something they weren't. People felt they were lied to, swindled out of money, and then got hurt, suffered in some other way or died in part because of this misrepresentation. Narconon and Scientology would deny any wrongdoing until the evidence proved otherwise in discovery, and after dragging it out as long as possible, every single lawsuit that I was aware of back then had settled out of court, until a more recent one in California that I wasn't involved in at all that ruled against Narconon after a trial. The main reason for the settlements was that they didn't want the evidence against them to be part of the permanent court record like many of the documents from the Georgia case that were filed. Most of what was found in discovery, including all of the depositions, were sealed as part of their settlements, and the dollar amounts were kept confidential. Scientology has deep enough pockets to pay, and my semi-educated estimate is that they paid out many tens of millions of dollars in Narconon cases alone, maybe more than a hundred million. When combined with other lawsuits against Scientology directly, the associated settlements are certainly into the hundreds of millions of dollars.

All of the criminal investigations fizzled out as well, that I'm aware of, as tracking down the individual responsible parties proved very difficult for them, and they were apparently unable to charge the organizations for many of the offenses. However, the Narconon network of programs in North America has been severely crippled. Almost all of the facilities have either changed modalities, shut down or reduced in size to be insignificant. The Georgia facility was shut down, as were the ones in Canada. One in Florida dissolved and another one changed its name and services and eventually closed as well. The ones in Northern California left the network and changed their program. The Oklahoma facility went from over 200 clients and 200 staff down to literally only a dozen or so of each, and is a relative ghost town. The ones in Southern California and Nevada shrunk dramatically. Louisiana shrunk. Michigan eventually closed. Their overall presence in the United States now is very tiny in comparison to how booming it was around 2005.

My personal goal was never to shut them all down, though I believe they deserved it because they refused to reform or be honest about who they were and what they were doing, but instead I wanted to speak the truth of what I knew and hold people accountable. I met many caring and talented people in Narconon and Scientology whom I would otherwise still consider friends. A lot of them also wound up finding their own ways out since then, though in a much quieter way. I also realize that there are as many ways to get well as there are people and that there are people who were helped by Narconon, but those choosing any particular form of help should get the full truth up front of what they're being exposed to and participating in. Informed consent should be common sense.

4. REBUILDING AND RECONNECTING

I reference several authors and some of their books throughout here that have had an impact on me in one way or another, and some of Michael Singer's work has presented itself to me in life a few different times. In his book *The Surrender Experiment: My Journey Into Life's Perfection*, he wrote, "*no matter who we are, life is going to put us through the changes we need to go through. The question is: Are we willing to use this force for our transformation? I saw that even very intense situations don't have to leave psychological scars, if we are willing to process our changes at a deeper level.*" Although it had been later for me chronologically when I actually read this book, it is very fitting for me while recounting parts of my life that have unfolded, including the rebuilding process. It has also taken me some more time to process different parts on deeper levels.

Before I moved back to Georgia, but still in

the middle of my departure from Narconon and Scientology, I had decided that I wanted to produce a documentary film about addiction and recovery. It was an ill-fated project that was partially tainted by many of the views I was in the middle of reconciling, but at the same time it also helped open the door for me to other people in the recovery field who didn't follow a mainstream agenda.

I had wanted to be involved in making movies for a long time, from taking acting classes when I was 19 and going on multiple auditions, to writing a script and trying to produce a feature film. Not much had panned out, but during the summer of 2011 I decided that I was going to do this video. I reached out to several people in the behavioral health and medical fields who seemed to challenge some of the status quo treatment models, or at least acknowledge that there could be other ways to get well, and about a dozen or so agreed to be interviewed. Two other people at first accepted, but later declined after they found out I had been involved in Narconon. They didn't want to be associated with that in any way, and I understood why.

A couple experts who did agree to speak with me on camera were Stanton Peele, PhD and Tom Horvath, PhD. Stanton wrote an acclaimed book called *7 Tools to Beat Addiction* and Tom Horvath was both the founder of a treatment program called Practical Recovery in La Jolla, CA, and the president of SMART Recovery, which is a free self help and support group for people. Both of these men had decades of experience, traditional degrees and training, and had a common sense approach that I was drawn toward. I learned a lot from them during our brief interactions. I flew myself and my camera man to New Jersey to interview Dr. Peele, which was a treat. I also flew out to southern California for a series of interviews, including driving down to La Jolla for the day to speak with Dr. Horvath and several of his therapists and counselors. One of his therapists used the word "mindfulness" in her interview, and it kept sticking in my head over the years as being the first place I recalled hearing it used in a recovery setting, and back then I didn't really understand what it meant.

The final version of the video, which I had titled *Curing Addiction*, showed that I had no clue what I was doing making a film at the time, but I was proud to have taken an idea and produced a feature length documentary that was largely self financed. Even though the production level was poor and a good portion of the content was shit, I was still happy to have accomplished it. The whole project turned out to basically be more of an expensive educational experience for me, and I had moved back to Georgia shortly after completing the final packaging for an attempt at distribution.

As a result of the loss of expected payments from selling my websites and the flop of a video I produced, I started to quickly burn through what little money I had left, and didn't have an immediate solution for a job. I was living off credit cards and maxed them out in just a couple months due to all of my expenses. Soon I had 40K in revolving debt and had to wind up borrowing another 60K on top of that. In just a matter of a few months I went from being owed 150K to being 100K in debt. A quarter of a million dollar swing was a huge hit. Things weren't looking good financially, but I was determined to pull out of it. I vowed to not just make a comeback, but to wind up far better than I had previously been, in every way.

After I started to publicly speak up, a few people whom I had known before wound up reaching out to me to talk, and one of them asked if I would work on his website. Having little to no income at the time, I gladly jumped at the opportunity and began helping his intervention company improve its rankings and traffic in Google. Mike Loverde, the owner, soon increased his budget and started to pay me a bit more. He also introduced me to several other treatment centers he worked with and recommended that they use my services, helping me land a few more clients. Before long, I was able to pay all of my own bills again and had steady work. I wasn't moving backwards anymore. I was relieved and reenergized, and I am grateful for Mike having taken a chance on me. I believe I would not have had that opportunity if I hadn't decided to speak out and become visible.

By the end of this period I was financially self-sufficient once again (though not out of debt), and I had regained a lot of pride and self respect in that regard. I was able to have a steady workload of a handful of treatment facilities that I did web work for, from content development and SEO to social media and some PR and marketing consulting.

In addition to finding more work, I was also able to start reconnecting with some other former associates and friends who had initially written me off, but then made their own way out of the mess.

One of them, Jeff Lukas, texted me out of the blue one day when I was in Minnesota for a family reunion. I still had his number saved, and we set up a time to talk after my trip. It turned out he was also working with Mike Loverde, and he had gotten my number from him (Narconon officials ordered many people to erase my number from their stored contacts) after he found out I was doing some work on his websites. Jeff and his wife Annie had been out for only a few months and had some trepidation about contacting me, but his curiosity and desire for connection and understanding were greater than his fears. They had been told how I was an evil person, but this conflicted with his past experiences and memories of our friendship and working relationship together. He had to find out for himself which was true - what he had been told, or what he experienced.

Jeff and I spoke for an hour or more on that first call, and it was so cathartic for both of us to begin to try and make sense of it all, both individual experiences and common themes. Being so heavily involved in those organizations was such a unique series of life events, and only someone else who had been through it could truly relate in detail. We were able to openly share our struggles of searching for normalcy while continuing to try to reconcile our past, and although he wasn't labeled an evil Suppressive Person like me, he was also cut off from a lot of people because he didn't leave on good terms - he and his wife had finally had enough and just walked away.

Jeff would turn out to be a key figure in my life, and he and Annie have been powerful symbols of bridging into the present and providing hope that more people would make it out of that trap. There have been several other "Jeffs" who have made it out, but he became much more than just reconnecting with an old friend, as we have worked together continuously for several years since then and have had more hour-long conversations than I could count about our understandings of the past, present and future. Eventually, our conversations become much more about life in general, such as work, kids, marriage, sports and anything else. Our friendship is way more authentic and meaningful now than it ever was back then.

One of the other people who also reached out to me was an original graduate of the Narconon program from the 1960's, and his name was Gordy Weinand. I had met Gordy many times over the years at different events in Oklahoma, California and Georgia, and he liked me and my parents because we were all originally from Minnesota. He had been involved early on for several years, but then was away for a long time, just living life. He was tracked down by a Narconon supporter and alumni from the '70s, who found he was living in Georgia and connected him up with Mary Rieser, the Scientologist who started the Narconon in Georgia.

Gordy and I had continued to stay in touch, although I didn't hear from him for a while as I was going through my exit. Then he called me one day and told me that he didn't care what anyone said, that he wasn't going to be told who he could be friends with. He said he knew I was a good person and that he considered me a friend. Gordy was never a Scientologist and therefore didn't get the deeper indoctrination that so many others had, despite his many years of support and service for and with Narconon.

Gordy was an example for me of someone who was truly conflicted with what to do regarding the organization. He desperately wanted to feel that his support over all the years wasn't done in vein, and that there was some good left in it somewhere. For him, the history from the beginning was meaningful, and his contribution was the personal connection he had with people, as of course there were some who did recover and appreciated their relationship with him. At the same time, he was furious with Mary Rieser and people at Arrowhead and Narconon International for all of the rest of the stuff. When a story on a local news station opened up with a picture of him from their website and then cut to police officers serving a warrant, he asked me what he could do about it. He specifically asked me for help writing a cease and desist letter to remove his likeness from any websites or other promotional materials. He sent them certified mail, but they were rejected. He told them in a couple phone calls, but his requests were ignored. Despite his anger and frustration with Narconon and Scientology, he still felt he owed an allegiance to some of his friends there as well, and he had no intention of cutting them out of his life, either. He stopped following through with his requests to be removed after things quieted down in the news.

Shortly after that, Narconon International was essentially dissolved and taken over by its parent organization in Scientology called the Association for Better Living and Education (ABLE), and of course Narconon Georgia was closed. Gordy went on to different work in semi-retirement doing product demonstrations at Sam's Club, and we would talk every other month or so to catch up and had lunch a couple of times. We both appreciated the continued contact and connection we had, including chatting about Minnesota teams like the Twins and the Vikings, and I was deeply saddened by his passing in October of 2018. I will always remember Gordy for his simple appreciation for friendships, his love for his family, and his personal drive to see people succeed in life, regardless of their chosen path.

As I continued my work with other treatment centers on a professional level, I was also consuming information through tons books on business, spirituality, non-dualism, psychology, sociology, self-help and other similar types of nonfiction. I started to see a pattern among them of shared views that were being presented or talked about in different ways. It was faint at first, but as the years go by this pattern continues to become more visible to me, and elements become more clear. I like to call them Universal Truths, and I don't believe that there is necessarily a finite number of them, as many are expressed in slightly different ways, and because things are constantly evolving. However, one that I did see early on was that if I continued to hold everyone connected to my past experiences in contempt, that not only would they likely never speak to me again, but I would not allow myself to be free. This became a fundamental component of my rebuilding process. I have had to forgive them and forgive myself and allow the space for people to reconnect. People like Mike and Jeff and Gordy were but a few examples of how this became a reality. To this day, I still hold a place in my heart for any of these people to re-enter my life in a new way, and some I even periodically send notes to via text, email or social media, to let them know that if they ever want to catch up over the phone or in person, that I leave the invitation open for them. I would love nothing more than for them to breathe the fresh air of freedom as well, and to know that the world is full of beautiful experiences and opportunities.

Letting go of the anger and distaste for them personally also allowed me to see things newly from a business perspective as well, and I found a renewed interest in the behavioral health field as a result, beyond just websites. I found many wonderful programs that were doing great work helping people, some that I worked with directly, and so many others out there that I've had only tangential contact with. I realized that there is no single right way to help someone, and that different programs work for different people, and at various times or circumstances in their lives.

Another key element for me has also been working on ridding myself of judgmental thoughts and actions as much as possible, and instead becoming more aware, accepting and inclusive. I have had to accept that my decisions and actions prior to now have gotten me exactly where I am today, and that there is meaning in all of it.

Many spiritual leaders and philosophers have shared the concept of togetherness, and even that we are all part of one greater universal life source. Scientific research of people and experiences have shown that there really is no separation in terms of energy - it is only perceived as such. Some experiments include proving concepts such as quantum entanglement and being able to affect change via thoughts, measurements and vibrations from a distance. In 2015, three scientists conducted separate experiments that showed two particles so distant from one another that no signal could connect them, even at the speed of light, nevertheless possessed an invisible and instantaneous connection.

They were awarded the prestigious Bell Prize from the University of Toronto for their work in quantum mechanics. Each and every person, living thing and inanimate object is made of the component parts of the universe and are all reliant upon and connected to each other. In that manner, reconnection is more about recognition, perception and understanding, as we are really never not connected. There is also a great scientific explanation of our interconnectedness of our heartbeats, breaths and matter in our brains from Tom Chi, co-founder of Google X. These commonalities in all people emanate from the same sources.

In another example of some of this research, there are multiple sources stating that the life expectancy of an individual is shortened when he or she harbors negative feelings toward another such as anger, and conversely, is lengthened when there is a sense of community, harmony and love. People who spend most of their lives being sad, angry, anxious or otherwise upset also tend to have more physical health problems as well, according to these studies.

Something I try to practice is to be aware whenever I have a negative thought or judgmental reaction to someone else's appearance or behavior, etc. I have to ask myself if there is something that is really unacceptable to me that they're doing, or is it something that is just different from what I would like or choose. Even the tagging the behavior as "bad" is a form of judgment in itself, though of course some things are more obvious than others.

is a good man.

Thankfully, he and my mom left Scientology as well, and they were there to help me get back on my feet when I needed them, financially and otherwise. Hopefully there is still time to reconnect on the level we had when I was much younger, even if it's not to the degree of the artists he works with. His dad passed away at 63, though, and my dad turns 63 in 2020, so who knows. I have resolved to be thankful for the moments we had in the past and the few we do have now, and try not to take it personally when I don't hear from him for weeks or sometimes even months. There are many people in this world who have had much less time with their fathers, or never knew their fathers, or had fathers who weren't kind to them or provided for them. I consider myself extremely lucky in that regard, and I am grateful for his love and contributions to my life as well.

I know that it's not fair to let my unmet expectations get in the way of sharing the moments we do have together. I know that if I really needed him in a crisis or something that he would of course be there, as he has been before. I have also been able to use my relationship with him as a learning experience in trying to be more present for my children and be mindful of continuing that as they grow older and become teenagers and adults. I get to kiss and hug and play with my boys pretty much every day, my daughter at least several days per month, and I try to talk to with her every day that we're not together. I want to have that level of contact with them that I wish I had with my dad, so that they know they can always talk to me about anything, and that I want to know what they're up to and be actively involved in their lives. I want to be able to provide for them as much emotional support for them as well.

Having the joy and privilege of being a father is something I am most proud of. Every action I take includes my family in the thought process, consideration or deliberation. This ranges from routine things like meals and schedules, but also for safety, education, experience, enjoyment, financial and career decisions, stress level and long-term goals. I can no longer make a purely selfish decision of any significance. The fact that I get to do things with my children and on their behalf is the greatest gift I have received in life.

we're not together. I want to have that level of contact with them that I wish I had with my dad, so that they know they can always talk to me about anything, and that I want to know what they're up to and be actively involved in their lives. I want to be able to provide for them as much emotional support for them as well.

Having the joy and privilege of being a father is something I am most proud of. Every action I take includes my family in the thought process, consideration or deliberation. This ranges from routine things like meals and schedules, but also for safety, education, experience, enjoyment, financial and career decisions, stress level and long-term goals. I can no longer make a purely selfish decision of any significance. The fact that I get to do things with my children and on their behalf is the greatest gift I have received in life.

is a good man.

Thankfully, he and my mom left Scientology as well, and they were there to help me get back on my feet when I needed them, financially and otherwise. Hopefully there is still time to reconnect on the level we had when I was much younger, even if it's not to the degree of the artists he works with. His dad passed away at 63, though, and my dad turns 63 in 2020, so who knows. I have resolved to be thankful for the moments we had in the past and the few we do have now, and try not to take it personally when I don't hear from him for weeks or sometimes even months. There are many people in this world who have had much less time with their fathers, or never knew their fathers, or had fathers who weren't kind to them or provided for them. I consider myself extremely lucky in that regard, and I am grateful for his love and contributions to my life as well.

I know that it's not fair to let my unmet expectations get in the way of sharing the moments we do have together. I know that if I really needed him in a crisis or something that he would of course be there, as he has been before. I have also been able to use my relationship with him as a learning experience in trying to be more present for my children and be mindful of continuing that as they grow older and become teenagers and adults. I get to kiss and hug and play with my boys pretty much every day, my daughter at least several days per month, and I try to talk to with her every day that

5. BELONGING, LOVE AND BRIGHTER FUTURES

Several years ago I was at my nephew's baseball game. There was a boy on his team who appeared to have Asperger's Syndrome, or possibly some other form of Highly Functioning Autism. On several occasions I remember seeing this young boy hopelessly go up to bat and strike out. Muffled groans emanated not so faintly from his teammates on the bench, but thankfully they were often drowned out by the cheering and encouragement from the boy's family, and other empathetic parents.

In each previous game I had watched, there was pretty much the same result when he was up to bat, which was him striking out and visible disappointment on his face and from his teammates. Occasionally he wouldn't swing at all and would get walked by the opposing pitcher, which was definitely a victory. I often observed the boy's father before, during and after his at-bats. I very distinctly remember feeling his pride, but it was sometimes muddied up by frustration, and then guilt for being frustrated. Afterwards it settled back in to just pure love, as if sometimes he realized that he may be projecting his hopes unfairly onto his son. At least this is what I was reading into it.

On this particular day, though, things were different. It was a back-and-forth game and both teams were charged up with excitement. It came time for them to bat again and they trailed by a couple runs. Soon it was this boy's turn to hit again, and one of his teammates loudly started cheering him on, shouting his encouragement. Other kids joined him, and the enthusiasm filled the bleachers as well. As the first pitch sailed toward home plate, the boy swung and connected solidly, sending the ball just over second base in a sharp line drive that nobody was expecting, especially the opposing team. The energy was electric. People were jumping up and down as the tying run scored - as if it were a scene in some ABC Family movie script or something.

I looked over at the boy's father and he could barely conceal his elation. The boy stood on base and looked for his dad in the crowd, and when he spotted him, he got that approving fist pump and smile that he so desperately wanted all season. I started crying on the spot and had to take a walk to dry my eyes. I think all children desperately want that approval from their parents and reassuring pride. It was such a beautiful moment, and I'm even overcome with emotion as I'm writing this now (and again each time I read it and re-experience that feeling).

They did wind up winning the game, and afterward, instead of the boy walking away with his head down silently or sitting off to the side, his chin was high and he had a smile on his face. Also, rather than his teammates barely noticing him, they all went out of their way to congratulate him. Hopefully some of those boys learned a lifelong lesson that day. That one at-bat changed his whole perception from being an outcast on his team to feeling like he belonged there, that he really was just like the other kids. That belonging is key, in my opinion, as well as encouragement and reassurance.

I have often struggled with feeling like I belonged anywhere, and that I have struck out many times and returned to sit on the bench. It still happens occasionally today. I have always been very comfortable when I am alone, while at the same time yearning for deeper connection with some person or group. Perhaps this is one reason why I love driving so much. I have had the good fortune of visiting 44 states thus far, and a fair amount of the travel was alone, either by plane or in the car. I have driven from coast to coast and many places in between. Although I am comfortable in groups and do well at events, I always look forward to a quiet sofa, the solitude of time on the toilet with a book to read (I'm thinking of starting a Twitter account called Toilet Seat Wisdom), or sitting at a desk or my kitchen island with my computer to read or write something. I didn't fully understand this dichotomy for a long time, and then I read Susan Cain's insightful book *Quiet: The Power of Introverts in a World That Can't Stop Talking*. It really explained so much for me and made a lot of sense. It also helped me believe I wasn't as abnormal as I thought. Despite being comfortable being alone, I didn't want to feel like I was all alone all the time. In a word, I wanted to feel like I belonged somewhere. I discovered that I first had to have a better understanding of myself to feel like I belonged anywhere.

This idea of belonging I think is central to many difficulties in self confidence and self love. I had to be comfortable in my own head, which built on the self esteem to feel like I belonged in various groups or circles. As I have continued to become more comfortable and more confident, I have also started to recognize and appreciate the connections I have by trying to develop a deeper sense of gratitude. This has led me to notice more good things that happen in my life day to day, and to not take as much for granted, as staying focused on the negative or bothersome things don't provide any benefit.

The recognition of and gratitude for people and circumstances in my life led to me deciding one day that I was going to ask Leslie to marry me. Up until that time, neither one of us were pushing for it. However, that day I drove down to a nearby jewelry store and picked out a stone and a setting and had something customized. I approached the purchase in a similar way to how I usually buy cars. I rarely just go to look - I intend on buying something! Of course this was much more significant of a purchase than a car, as I was making a conscious decision to make our love for each other more officially recognized. I was able to pick up the ring from the jeweler in time to propose on her birthday in November 2014. I was trying to think of a clever and romantic way to ask her to marry me, but I'm just not that graceful and couldn't hide my excitement. So, almost immediately after she walked in the door getting home from work that night, with our son Rhett fussing in the background in his jumper wanting to be picked up, I proceeded. My voice cracked as I tried to talk and fought back tears down on one knee, but I was eventually able to get the words out, or at least the ring and the posture indicated what I was trying to say. Even though it wasn't romantic, it was definitely a surprise, and it was perfect.

We decided that we didn't want to have a long engagement, and that we didn't want it to be too hot or too cold, so we picked the middle of April as the target date for our wedding.

Five months later I was standing on a hillside on a sunny Saturday afternoon in the middle of a vineyard in Dahlonega, GA. I leaned over to talk to the man who was about to perform our wedding ceremony. Just two weeks earlier, Ken wasn't even an ordained officiant and didn't know he would be standing there in that capacity, but instead thought he and his wife, Beth, were simply going to be our guests. I was already starting to get really emotional and the ceremony hadn't even started, but I also felt completely comfortable, as if it was all meant to be.

I can't say that I am a huge believer in fate, as I feel that we have so much influence over what directions our lives wander in, but there have been times like this that I can't explain as anything else other than the Universe at work. We were meant to be there.

The first person who was supposed to perform the ceremony had fallen off a ladder and broke his ankle only a couple weeks before the wedding. We were crushed, as we were really looking forward to having him out. However, after things settled out a bit, Leslie called up Ken, who was actually her boss at the time, and he graciously accepted and jumped in with both feet.

Aside from the part that Ken did an absolutely amazing job as our officiant, there were many elements that seemed to be fulfilling some kind of destiny. When too many incredible things line up, they are more than mere coincidences, in my book. Call it Divine intervention, synchronicity, the stars aligning or some other way to explain it, but the whole event was way more than luck. It was supposed to happen just the way it was.

First of all, the venue we chose, Montaluce, was normally booked up about a year in advance, but the exact date we wanted happened to be the only one that was left for the whole season. We really wanted to rent out the entire venue because it was so beautiful, but it was too expensive for our budget. Then, after we committed, they wound up giving us the whole place anyway, rather than just the private party spaces. The band we wanted (Chris Weaver) was originally booked up and supposed to be out of the country that week, but the date became available a few weeks before and they agreed to do it. It was also raining for several days leading up to the wedding, even pouring down heavily as were driving up for the rehearsal and barbecue we had planned. As we got closer to Dahlonega, the rain slowed and the clouds weren't as dark. Then it stopped raining as we pulled in to the villas where the party was going to be, and just before rehearsal, the clouds parted to reveal blue skies and sunshine. The weather turned out to be beautiful that evening and all day on Saturday for the wedding, and then the rain returned by Sunday morning.

I had also mentioned to Ken before the ceremony that the number eleven was a very significant number for both Leslie and me. Our birthdays are in the 11th month, which is also when we got engaged, and it just so happened that we were married on the 11th day of April. Ken told me that the number eleven had always been a special number for him and his wife was well, and Ken's birthday was the same day as Leslie's.

The whole event probably couldn't have gone better, from the venue and weather to the friends and family who joined us, and all of the other parts that came together to make it a magical weekend. It was definitely a very special experience that always invokes warmth and love when I think about it or go back and look at pictures, which were beautifully captured on film by an amazing photographer.

Love is the purest, most beautiful sentiment that exists in the universe. There are so many different forms of love and there is an infinite amount of it. It can be freely given without fear of it ever running out. I found that I had to be willing to give *and* receive love in order to find it, otherwise the pathway was blocked. I feel that sometimes there are things in the way that can cause detours, and that if we're open to it, then we may just find out that the unexpected path is the one that we are supposed to be on at that time anyway.

As we keep building our life together, I continue to gain confidence and appreciate life more, both through the very difficult times and the blissful moments. The more love I feel, the more I notice is prevalent in the world. It is a testament to attracting similar vibrations, and to brighter futures ahead.

6. FINDING MEANING

One of the most referenced books in history, and one often credited with providing inspiration or guidance, is Viktor Frankl's *Man's Search for Meaning.* Frankl was a psychiatrist from Austria who survived several Nazi prison camps in World War II, and later documented his experiences. What he found was that people who felt that their life had meaning were more likely to survive, even under such unimaginably horrific conditions as the Holocaust. Additionally, he developed Logotherapy to provide a way for people to transform their suffering, no matter how light or how severe, and turn it into something positive.

The fact that we all suffer in different ways throughout our time is a bond that we share, and a way for us to empathize with each other. Looking for the meaning that can be derived out of our individual hardships can be a transformative exercise, as I have come to personally experience. At the same time, when we have triumphant events and experiences that we share with others, it helps us relate better and have a greater sense of meaning and belonging as well.

Reading this book has had a lasting impact on me. As I continued to make more connections, reconnect with other people and build confidence and optimism, I had the thought that it was entirely possible that everything I had been through had provided me with the tools and experience I needed for my next chapters in life. I began finding meaning in the suffering I had endured, that the enforced isolation and spiritual torture had a purpose as an existential lesson for me. Once I was free from the mental prison that I was keeping myself locked in for so long, I feel like I became both softer and more resilient at the same time. I realized I had the keys all along, and I have been learning how to use them more and more to open new doors.

The good experiences have also had meaning and purpose. As I continued working with various treatment centers throughout the country on a consulting basis and kept on studying for myself, I found out more about the good works happening in the mental health and substance abuse treatment fields, and was able to identify some things I thought were lacking as well. I saw additional opportunities to help people also free themselves from their own prisons.

Along the long journey climbing back out of the pit of despair I found myself in, I continued reading a ton of books, watching TED talks, and consuming other forms of audio and video content about self improvement, happiness in life, success in business, sociology, psychology, spirituality, and more, in addition to the books that I was reading.

Perhaps one person who spoke to me as much as any other individual was Jon Kabat-Zinn. He is the founder of the Mindfulness Based Stress Reduction (MBSR) program, which is a well defined and systematic patient-centered educational approach that uses relatively intensive training in mindfulness meditation as the core of a program to teach people how to take better care of themselves and live healthier and more adaptive lives. The first program was developed in the Stress Reduction Clinic at the University of Massachusetts Medical Center in the '70s. His books *Full Catastrophe Living* and *Wherever You Go, There You Are* were very eye opening for me and remain among the ones I recommend the most. Another book by his colleague Saki Santorelli called *Heal Thyself: Lessons on Mindfulness in Medicine* left its mark on me as well. The healing powers of the mind and spirit on the physical body are tremendous and serve as wonderful aides to traditional medicine, and where appropriate, as the primary treatments themselves.

Sometimes people equate mindfulness only with Eastern religions, because that is where it started, but the applications and definitions have grown over time, and the MBSR program and similar uses are not religious practices in terms of being exclusively tied to, nor excluded from, any particular form of religion. Mindfulness isn't just a buzzword, either. After my previous religious experiences, I had zero interest in any belief systems or dogma. What struck me in part was that this form of being aware in the present moment non-judgmentally was so simple, yet had incredible effects for me right away. Kabat-Zinn has spent time with great Eastern religious leaders, yet he has a PhD in molecular biology from MIT, and the roots of the program started in a hospital working with patients battling all sorts of chronic conditions. This spiritual framework coupled with scientifically measurable application was appealing. Mindfulness and meditation are centering practices for me to be more calm, more accepting and more focused, and there are many forms and teachers and methods, from sitting meditations to mindful movement, Yoga, guided meditations and more. I feel like I am able to have a richer experience of life simply by paying attention and appreciating it more, as I continue to become more aware of myself and the world around me. It is a personal thing that I can keep practicing at any time, not just through meditation but also in everyday activities and experiences. I have found that being more mindful throughout the day produces a feeling of being more alive and engaged instead of just going through motions or tumbling through life. It also helps me to self-correct faster and with less effort when I misstep along the way.

Eventually my personal studies and treatment

center consulting work intersected. Some old contacts opened up a new treatment facility in the Florida panhandle, and I was brought on as a consultant to help them do some web development, public relations and create a place for themselves in the market. I also did some training with their local marketing company, which was new to the behavioral health space. They wound up doing really well getting off the ground, and then they ended the contract after a couple of years, once they felt they were self-sufficient. I had stayed in touch with one of the guys who as involved on and off, and let him know that if he ever wanted to do something truly unique and start his own thing, to give me a call sometime. His name was Reed Smith, and he and I spoke every now and then to keep updated on how things were going with them and with trends in the field. Eventually there came a time where he felt he was limited in his role there, and he and his wife, Krista, were interested in exploring other options where they could have ownership and more creative control on the programming and overall direction.

My experience complimented theirs well, as Reed was an intake person and Krista was just finishing a psychology degree, and they both enjoyed teaching classes and running groups. We also had similar talents that overlapped in some areas, but essentially we each had our specialties and started talking about what a partnership might look like. We came to a basic agreement and I began looking at properties in Georgia. Initially, we thought we were going to open a boutique residential treatment facility. I looked at properties such as old event places, old motels, higher-end homes, and even an old elementary school, but the more properties I looked at and the more zoning barriers I ran into, we decided to go with the route that had the best potential to prove our concept and grow from there. It was also the least expensive route to go and the path with the least resistance and risk for opening.

We decided to call it Centered Recovery Programs, and we wanted it to be a mindfulness-based program that was different from anything else out there. After all, by then there were plenty of facilities that incorporated a bit of Yoga or meditation, but none that we were aware of that really used mindfulness and thought detachment as the foundation for the whole program. It was going to be a collection of our combined experiences mixed with traditional therapies, and an evolving curriculum developed and compiled by Krista that was backed by a volume of research from other sources and that grew over time as it was put into practice at our program. It continued to take shape and is a series of some of the Universal Truths I previously mentioned, taken from many different sources and packaged into a consumable format for people looking to improve their lives. The way it is all put together, with solid evidence-based practices, is definitely unique.

Having settled on starting with an outpatient program, the fact still remained that roughly 90% of the people who get help each year do so through outpatient services. So my months-long property search turned to looking at mixed use facilities, professional office spaces and medical buildings. Even though there were many more of these types of properties available in our market, finding one that would fit our needs and budget requirements still proved to be difficult. Not only did we need additional parking, a mid-size space and proper zoning, we had very little money to put down and were faced with the hurdle of being considered a less than desirable tenant as well as having no business history since we were a start-up. I spent months looking at dozens of properties online and in person. Sometimes a simple drive-by and look in the windows would be sufficient, while other times it meant meeting our Realtor and engaging in discussions with landlords. Overall, I looked at properties in Cartersville, Acworth, Kennesaw, Woodstock, Canton, Roswell, Alpharetta, Marietta and other cities north of Atlanta. It was quite a process. I kept running into a lot of dead ends, but I wasn't willing to give up, because I had resolved to see this through to the end or regret not doing it for the rest of my life. This was going to work, I was sure of it. I could *feel* it. I knew it was something I needed to do, just like marrying Leslie.

I finally found a place in Roswell, GA that was owned by a larger company who was willing to give us a shot. I had a good feeling about the property, and had hoped that one of the doctors in the complex would be willing to serve as our Medical Director as well. They figured that the space had been empty for a while and we might as well get a chance to do something there. They even agreed to put up the money for our renovations and spread it out over the course of our lease, and also to give us the first three months free while we waited for the State Department of Community Health to grant our license and become operational. We all had to sign personal guarantees, provide a business description and ensure we would adhere to the standards of the other tenants in the complex, who were all healthcare providers of some type. We also wound up having a conference call with their leasing manager in Virginia to introduce ourselves and let him ask us questions. He wanted us to guarantee that we weren't like a previous tenant they had in another one of their properties - which happened to be none other than Narconon of Georgia! *I mean, what were the chances?* I actually laughed on the phone when he asked if I'd heard of Narconon, which created a bit of an awkward pause, and then I assured him that we were nothing like them, and that I was actually involved, to some degree, in the lawsuits and state investigations that got them shut down. All of that seemed to be compelling enough for them to let us go ahead with the lease and have the renovations completed so we could open.

Reed and Krista came up and found a house to buy in the area and we finalized the lease and got the facility renovations under way. I was lucky enough for Leslie to agree to move from Kennesaw to Roswell, as she was committed to helping in her capacity as the fourth owner as well. She knew I had to do this, and endured a lot in support of the project, which is an understatement. Throughout my time living in Georgia I had always wanted to live in the North Fulton areas of Roswell, Milton or Alpharetta. Turns out we were able to find a house in Roswell on the Milton border, and the office had a Roswell address but was actually under the City of Alpharetta jurisdiction.

While all of this was going on, we were about to have another baby boy, and his original due date was supposed to be April 11th - on our anniversary! There's that number eleven again.

Things were getting a little tight, but I was just as excited as I was nervous. It was like there was enough inertia to push things along and the steps on the pathway were already laid for us to keep going, we just had to keep walking. Our home in Kennesaw went under contract in less than two weeks for nearly the full asking price, which was a huge relief since we wouldn't have been able to afford both homes for very long. We were cutting it really close on several timelines though, and it was a challenge, to say the least, as well as additional stress. We moved into our new home on April 3rd, and then our son Max was born on April 7th! We spent the next few months just trying to get settled and acclimated to the new area and having a new routine (although having a new baby is anything but routine). Thankfully, my consulting business with Jeff was doing really well that summer and we were working with some great programs, so that took some of the added financial stress off, if only for a bit. Although Leslie had a wonderful job that paid really well, I didn't want her to feel like the majority of the financial burden was going to be hers.

Reed and Krista moved their family up in June, and then the renovations on our facility were finished the first week of July. We officially took possession of the property on July 5th, and by then we had already filed our application with the state and were just waiting on them to schedule our inspection so that we could begin seeing clients. Two months after we had initially filed our application, we finally got a call from one of the state employees, who said she could fit us in the following Monday. At the office that day, we were really nervous, and I was sweating profusely. Here we were opening our first program together, with a lot riding on the line. None of us had been through this by ourselves, so we didn't know exactly what to expect. However, by the end of the day on July 31st 2017, we had passed our inspection and were told we could begin providing services - Centered Recovery Programs was officially open by August 1st, and it took us three weeks to get our first client.

There were several things along the way that felt like the Universe was sending us messages that we were on the right path, and to keep going, in addition to the housing situation. The first doctor in the medical complex we approached to be our Medical Director agreed, as his private office was in the building next door and it was convenient for him to do exams for us. Our first client paid up front for several weeks' worth of treatment, and was happy to be getting extra attention from all of our staff. A contact of Reed's agreed to pay the salary for one of our contractors, Mayer Harris, for six months before we had to start paying him, so it was like getting a free employee for a while, although we paid for his hotel and then his apartment while he commuted each week from Alabama. Mayer turned out to be a very reliable team member for over a year and a half, before he eventually decided to stay in Alabama. We also had an Australian psychologist call up one day named Bridgett Spicer. She told me she just moved here and lived around the corner, had a background in mindfulness practices, was becoming a certified Yoga instructor, and wanted to know if she could volunteer for a few hours per week until she was able to be employed in the U.S. We heartily agreed and were very grateful for her participation as well. There were several other staff who felt like they were meant to be with us, including Allison, Colin and Mike, in their respective roles along the way. Most of the therapists we hired were part-time, which allowed them to work in their private practices and/or with other groups as well. Pieces simply fit well together.

Between the renovation costs being amortized over the life of our lease, some free or low-cost staff help, some donated items, and the fact that Reed,

Krista and I did all that we could ourselves in the beginning, we were able to get the facility open and running for even less than we had initially anticipated. This turned out to be needed, because right after we opened, Google hampered the ability for treatment centers to advertise by blocking terms on AdWords that were specific to this field, citing a handful of predatory program operators. We also wound up having a large insurance carrier sit on claims for months before finally getting us uploaded into their system to be able to process them so we could receive payment.

Things got really tight for a while, as we were still an unknown entity and we had to pivot from our original marketing plans and learn to network better on a local level. It was something that we weren't really used to previously. More help arrived, though, just when we needed it. A friend of Reed's had some money to invest and gave us a small cash injection that helped cover some bills, and also Jeff and I were able to sell some websites that made it so I didn't need to draw a salary for the rest of 2017 and all of 2018. Meanwhile, things were picking up, clients were coming in and getting help, and the claims for those clients who had insurance were finally starting to be paid. I was already looking for our next location and pushing for it, but it took some persistence to get everyone else on board with moving in that direction already within the first 12 months of operation. I specifically remember a Board meeting we had in April of 2018, where it seemed like I was the only one ready to act. Part of my role was to predict, plan and develop strategies for growth, and it was tough at times to get enough agreement to move forward with some of those plans. Thankfully, the updated numbers I was predicting did start to show, and by June we all agreed to start officially looking for our next location.

Finding the right real estate was challenging from the beginning, and the second facility wasn't much easier. We had many hurdles again where landlords didn't want our type of business there, regardless of the glowing report we had from the landlord at our first location. The building we ultimately found in Marietta had an old zoning stipulation that wasn't found until we went to get the paper signed off by Cobb County, even after they had given us verbal approval prior to signing the lease. This set us back several weeks while the landlord had to have the stipulation removed from the record in a public hearing to be able to allow for other types of businesses to operate from there. This then opened the door for us to be able to occupy the space in September, and we were able to complete our cosmetic enhancements in preparation for opening. I wound up putting in a considerable amount of physical work into getting it ready, including a lot of painting, carpet cleaning, putting together all of the furniture and spreading a truckload of landscaping rocks. I remember standing in the parking lot one day prior to opening, and just taking a moment to acknowledge all that had gone into creating the program and company and its progress, and feeling a real sense of pride in how far we'd come in such a relatively short period of time. The Marietta facility officially opened after its inspection on November 1, 2018, just 15 months after our first location opened.

Thankfully I had pushed hard enough to get the second facility open, because in October there was a pipe that burst in the empty suite above us in Roswell over a weekend, and water gushed down and flooded out our entire office. We got a call from the fire department on a Sunday morning saying that water was coming out from under the doors into the parking lot. I grabbed Rhett and hurried out the door, hoping that the damage wouldn't be too bad. By the time I got there Reed and Krista had already been inside. Reed looked at me and said, "It's all gone." For a moment I wasn't sure if he was serious, because he has a really dry sense of humor, but when I noticed there was not even a hint of a smile in his eyes, my heart sank. I fought back tears as I looked over at my son, who was sitting on the curb that chilly morning being entertained by a kind firefighter who was pointing to different things on the fire truck and had offered him a hat. *How could this be happening?* At that moment, I realized that I had to be strong and stay positive and instill the message that everything was going to be okay, both for my family and my coworkers. Our combined resolve was too great to let this sack us completely.

We then spent the next few hours wading

through ankle-deep water trying to salvage anything we could, but there was so much water that had come down from above that the ceiling continued to collapse, and even many of the things we thought we could save wound up being too damaged after all. Each time we re-entered the facility more pieces of drywall were falling, lighting fixtures were dangling and insulation was everywhere. It was a very surreal day, and we had to keep moving forward, otherwise it was easy to get caught up into thinking that our business had just been destroyed.

Optimism and determination paid off, because just a couple weeks later our new office was licensed and we stayed alive. We had to transfer out most of our clients and practically start over, but we had a strong team and had developed a great reputation locally in the treatment community. It took forever for the various insurance companies to pay for things, but they eventually did. The landlord's policy paid for a complete rebuild, and we wound up having an even nicer facility than before, but it took 16 weeks to reopen. We also had business interruption coverage and business personal property coverage so we were able to replace all of the physical items and a decent portion of our lost revenue. We weathered a major storm that would have crippled many small businesses, especially those still in their infancy. By the first of March of 2019, both facilities were open full-time and have been doing really well ever since.

One of the best parts of the business model

we created made it almost resistant to market fluctuations. In other words, as being a true outpatient program, we were able to offer services to local residents at much more affordable prices than going away to inpatient treatment, when the levels of care were appropriate, and we also developed great relationships with residential facilities, detox centers and other treatment professionals. By having a unique focus, people who were looking for something different were naturally putting us high on their list of alternatives. Then, when people really started to experience shifts in their daily lives, the positive reviews and strong reputation continued to spread.

I had been working to get systems created and in place and encouraging Reed and Krista to do so as well, so that it could keep growing with or without any of the co-founders having to be present. The program has the capacity to become the nationally-recognized leader in non-12 step recovery, including offering free peer support group meetings, online services and a growing number of locations.

Even though there continued to be plenty of challenges, starting Centered Recovery Programs really was a dream come true in many ways, and something that I felt I had to be a part of and accomplish. I had initially had an idea about creating something in Georgia back in 2005, but then tabled that until I was actually ready to follow through with it. It took getting another dozen years of experience under my belt and having the mindset, resources and support to pull it off, as well as partners who were ready to do so as well. For me, the challenge and excitement of taking something from an idea phase, to an actual business proving the concept, replicating it, and then preparing it for exponential growth is very exciting to me. It made it that much better to be in a field that is helping transform lives every day.

At the start of the Fall in 2019 I had determined that it was time to cease my active role in the company, as I felt we had reached the end of our ability to walk the path together. After some back and forth, I had a call scheduled with my attorneys on November 11th at 11 AM (there they are again, coincidentally), and I decided then that I was going to accept their last offer for me to let them have full control over the company. I have tremendous respect for the work they have done and are continuing to do, and I wish them the very best on their continued journey, and look forward to seeing how far it goes.

I have also continued working with Jeff with Advanced Recovery Resources by offering help to individuals, families and treatment centers. Now we have even more experience under our belts and are able to help in more ways. We provide a wide range of services, from online resources, interventions and recovery support services, to consulting for programs in the areas of admissions, marketing, management and strategic planning. I started putting more time and effort into consulting projects through this company again after exiting Centered, and have had the opportunity to once again work with a number of great programs and people in the recovery field. I'm excited to see what other opportunities present themselves.

I am proud to be able to work in the behavioral health space with quality programs and professionals. There is no way I would have been able to be a part of making these happen and contribute to people's lives in such a manner had I not endured what I did earlier in my life. My earlier experiences, and the suffering I endured, put me in a position to do many things as a result. I would not have had the courage to take action, the determination to see ideas and concepts become reality, or the strength and confidence to help forge these new paths for others as well. I also wouldn't have been able to overcome some of the struggles or act quickly without taking loss personally, and I likely wouldn't have even been in this field at all had I not been sent to Oklahoma in 1998 by my parents.

7. OVERCOMING STRUGGLES

Although most things in life have been going really well for me, I have certainly been met with many challenges and difficulties along this new path. In addition to the personal adjustment of trying to make sense of everything that was happening and create a new life, there have been plenty of other obstacles, some of which I still have to continually deal with.

Professionally, it has been tough trying to stick with plans even when the course changes along the way. Taking these curve balls in stride have helped to sharpen my abilities as well as strengthen my resolve and improve my vision and strategic planning, though I have many lingering bruises still. For example, having to pivot in the beginning stages of Centered and during the flood were dramatic and definitely intense. There were many weeks early on where I wasn't sure where money was going to come from, and had to pay staff out of my personal savings on more than one occasion. My job was to make sure people had what they needed to do their jobs, and to keep looking forward, and it was often a thankless portion of behind-the-scenes entrepreneurship that a lot of people don't see or even realize. On the upside, it also helped me gain new skills and knowledge that I can build on.

When I exited Centered, it wasn't yet at the point that I was originally hoping for, but the timing still felt right nonetheless. In the same year, an attempt to open a different program in Pittsburgh with Jeff struggled to get off the ground due to unforeseen family situations he had to deal with, and I lost all of my investment in it. I had also bought a stock that completely tanked, losing nearly all of its value, and I invested in a small farm that didn't meet expectations for the year due to technicalities and market fluctuations of their product. Needless to say, my income goals for that time period were nowhere near what I had set out to accomplish. And yet at the same time, I had tremendous success and learned so much about myself, business, what to do different for future ventures and how to be able to help others by teaching them things that worked for me as well as what to avoid. I've had some pretty dramatic swings in my income over the years. I know a lot of people would prefer the predictability and stability of a regular paycheck, and I'm extremely grateful that Leslie is one of those people, but I personally love the excitement of doing new things, expanding ideas and starting up companies.

On a more personal level, fighting for my parental rights with my daughter and trying to keep her as safe as possible from a distance has been a big struggle for many years. I do have to remain vigilant to protect her against any negative influence from Scientology, but hopefully one day that will no longer be a threat. Although I am so thankful that we get to see her as often as we do and that she gets to spend time with our family here in Georgia pretty much every month, it rips me to pieces on the inside having to say goodbye to my child each time and not being able to see her for several weeks. Of course this is something that all divorced parents must got through to some degree, and I realize that, but it doesn't really make it easier. I still cry every time I hear the words, "I wish I didn't have to go." All I can do is hug her and tell her I wish she didn't have to go either, that she'll be back soon, and that I love her. This has been going on for eight years now, and it honestly doesn't get any easier to say goodbye.

There is also the continual challenge of trying to balance a blended family as well. I try to be conscious of how much affection is shown to each of my children and my wife as well as how our time is spent together. As with many other personal difficulties, it is hard to describe how tough this can be sometimes unless someone else has also had to navigate a similar situation. It is hard for everyone involved. The blessing side is of course that I did get another chance and that I do have a wonderful family. Each of us are still learning our roles and how everything fits into place, year after year, or we try to find new ways of doing things and fulfill those roles the best we can. It is certainly confusing for the boys since they don't yet understand the situation and wonder why Ella leaves for weeks at a time and then is back for a few days. Thankfully, there are some holidays and summer schedules where we all get to spend more time together for a solid week or more, and we get closer to settling into a new routine.

A few years ago there was a very rough time when we had back-to-back miscarriages and several illnesses in the family, including hand, foot and mouth as well as mono. At one point we were just barely making it through the day, trying our best to eat and rest and regain our health, as all three were a challenge. Neither Leslie nor I could sleep for more than a few minutes at a time because we couldn't stop coughing, despite the best prescription-strength cough medicine we could find and plenty of over the counter aids as well. Continual fatigue, aching and an inability to be anywhere comfortable for any length of time magnified everyday challenges. Since I didn't get it as bad, I was then tasked with taking Rhett to and from school and watching him the majority of time when he was home for a period of time.

Leslie got hit the hardest. All her fingernails fell off from the hand, foot and mouth that Rhett brought home from his preschool. She coughed so much and was so uncomfortable from the mono that one week I literally put a mattress on the floor in a basement room that had no light and she had a vaporizer, lots of medicine, a glass of water and a box of tissues. She was so tired yet couldn't sleep. It was a nightmare for us, but especially for her.

Then there was the first miscarriage, which was definitely more traumatic than the second. We had already told our parents and were excited about having another baby, but when we went in for an ultrasound they found that the heartbeat was slow. I distinctly remember being confused and panic started to set in after we were told that there was a very slim chance that the baby would survive. There was nothing we could do to change it. We had to monitor it closely and go back in a week, which seemed like one of the longest weeks of our lives, to see if there was any improvement. Several times each day we would pause and think about whether or not the fragile little baby embryo striving to grow would make it. The suspense, anxiety and sadness over the potential loss was killing us.

We went back in the next week and our fears were confirmed. There was no heartbeat detected. We had lost the baby. Nothing could have really prepared us for the loss that we felt. Kind of like the first time I got the wind knocked out of me, yet on an emotional level. It didn't matter how many stories about this happening we had read or heard about, nor the doctor telling us what percentages of pregnancies miscarry, we weren't really prepared. It hurt, and it took a while to recover from. We had already built up the stories in our heads about the baby before we got the sad news, and now everything that we were dreaming about was suddenly gone. I can't imagine what it would be like for parents to lose their children after they were born, other than it must be exponentially more heart wrenching, and I feel terrible that people have to endure such loss.

Not much later, Leslie was pregnant again, but this time we were much more cautious and guarded about it. We knew not to tell anyone else yet, and that we had to go in to see the doctor. Leslie had mentioned that she didn't feel pregnant like she did before. When we made it in to see the doctor, the hunch was confirmed. The second miscarriage was less traumatic, as the embryo turned out to be empty. It was still a loss that we had to deal with, though, and started to fuel thoughts that maybe we wouldn't be able to have any more children. More worry, more anxiety, less certainty about life and the future of our family, or if we even wanted to try again only to go through more heartache. I now know a sliver of the heartache that many families go through who struggle with infertility.

However, the more we talked about it with people, the more stories we heard from friends and family members who had gone through miscarriages of their own. What was comforting wasn't that someone else had suffered, but that most of them all had gone on to have healthy children afterward, even those who had multiple miscarriages as well. Still, we were cautious, but ultimately decided we still wanted to try. Then, Leslie became pregnant in mid-2016 again, and when we went for the first appointment the baby had a strong heartbeat, and the due date was supposed to be our anniversary. We knew this time would be different. We had genetic testing done since Leslie was over the age of 35, and found out right away that we were having another boy! On the plus side, the baby was healthy and growing, but Leslie wound up being extremely nauseous the entire time. The trade off now was that she was really sick, and that he was also very strong, and nearly broke her ribs on more than one occasion. It really took a toll on her.

Our second son, Max, was born on April 7th 2017. The delivery was great, up until a few hours afterward, where Leslie had pretty severe clotting and hemorrhaging. We had several nurses in the room trying to assist, and they were able to eventually help stabilize everything and prevent her from having to get a blood transfusion. I felt helpless trying look into Leslie's eyes and let her know that she was going to be okay, and that Max was okay. No doubt the look on my face wasn't very comforting, but I was doing my best to remain calm, despite at one point being very fearful that she wasn't going to make it through the night. What was supposed to be a restful room where we could get acclimated with our newest family addition turned out looking and sounding like a horror movie for a couple of hours, and we were in shock the rest of the time in the hospital. We couldn't wait to get the hell out of there the next day and get home. Again, I was thankful to make it through with everyone's basic health intact.

The next challenge, not to mention all that comes with moving and trying to open a new business, was the sleep deprivation over the following year. It was more than I had ever experienced prior to that, and I often felt like I was near a breaking point. I was up every night with Max, often multiple times, then up early with Rhett and then off to work. Despite being lucky enough to also have childcare help during the day, neither Leslie nor I were getting any serious rest. We had the new house, the new baby, the new business, plus trying to keep up with other work and kids. Pretty much all parents of newborns go through some form of this, but it seemed especially hard, possibly because of the other demands, and possibly because I was facing my forties and had the thinning hair and pot belly to prove it. At times it seemed like there just wasn't a way to catch up, on sleep or in life, and we did our best to plod ahead and be grateful, even with the dark circles under our eyes.

The most recent situation involved a surgery that Leslie had. Something had been building in her for years from being hard on herself and very driven to succeed, having a high pressure job, a near-fatal car accident, to surgery for melanoma, her own prior divorce, and then miscarriages and illnesses, a very difficult pregnancy and this last surgery, and her body sent her a very clear message that she needed some time to heal. There wasn't ever enough time in between to fully regain the necessary strength, it seemed. Instead of it being a succession of individual events, it turned out to be more like a compound of all of them together over a number of years that was more than any person should have to endure.

It wound up being a very difficult time, especially with the lack of sleep we were experiencing, but every time I felt like I couldn't take it anymore, I had to remind myself that it was even more difficult for her. Despite all that she has been through, she continued to show up and be present and keep up with obligations at work and at home. Sometimes I feel really selfish complaining about having my own struggles knowing that she's had to deal with much more, and I try to remind myself of the power of being grateful for all that is, and how that can really help provide strength and positivity now and in the future.

Internally, I struggle with the pressure I put on myself to live up to a set of ideals that are often unfair to me and people around me. On one hand I expect peace, love, happiness, success and fulfillment, while on the other I feel that they are only fleeting moments. I have to be careful with knowing the difference between having goals and being dissatisfied with all that has already been achieved. I have to remind myself to be more thankful of the wonderful experience of being a parent rather than focusing on the difficulty of dealing with a tantrum of a small child. I have to be grateful for the abundance that already is in our lives in so many ways instead of whishing we had more.

These are mental traps that many of us fall into. I am learning to be more appreciative and enjoy all of these moments, the blissful and the heartache, the fun and the irritating, the pleasure and the pain, and in doing so I do find myself having a more enriched experience of living. At times I am willing to give everyone else the benefit of the doubt, yet I refuse to give myself a break, let alone be congratulatory for things I've done that I should be proud of. As the opening line of my personal website says, "welcome to a work in progress."

There was a time when Leslie and I were seeing a therapist together, and he had indicated he detected some anxiety in me, too. Despite my initial rejection of such an idea, I knew deep down he was absolutely right. This led me to revisit what I thought was possibly a spiritual experience as a teenager, where I was unable to walk straight or focus my eyes enough to drive and I wept uncontrollably, shaking. My friend dropped me off at home where I collapsed on the floor and eventually passed out, completely sober. The next morning my mom found me on the floor and asked what happened, but I struggled to explain. I now believe this could have been a panic attack. I have a tendency to hold in too much for too long, and I can get wound really tightly until a string finally snaps, or bottled up until enough pressure creates an explosion. I've had to become more aware of this and find additional ways to allow things and people to be as they are, to find ways to unwind or release the pressure valve and to settle back closer toward a state of equanimity.

For most of the challenges I have faced and continue to find myself in the middle of, when I step back I see that there is more than a silver lining, for these are also blessings, and there are certainly people who have it far worse in every way. I have to refocus on the positives to otherwise not get lost in the inherent sadness or suffering I experience or witness. I can acknowledge their weight on my heart as it empties, yet still feel the love and warmth that comes rushing back in. Gratitude outweighs the despair. Love and a feeling of innate wholeness drowns out fear.

Sometimes I think about my personal, familial or work difficulties and how much has been accomplished and also how wonderful life has been in spite of it, or rather *because* of it. Most people had little to no clue about the daily struggles, and this helps me realize that others are the same way - most people have their own difficult situations in life that they're dealing with on any given day, and I need to try and give them a break as well. If they have young children, they've probably recently dealt with a tantrum. They have probably had some argument or disagreement at home or at work. Maybe they have a health condition, or lost a loved one recently, or are financially strained. Maybe all of these, or more.

When I'm feeling too down or frustrated with something in life, I often have to pull myself away from what I'm doing and take a break. I specifically try to do something completely opposite of what I'm working on, such as taking a walk outside, going for a drive or a household chore if I've been stuck in my head staring at the computer, on the phone too long or caught up in a problem.

By refocusing my attention elsewhere, it opens my mind up for thoughts to flow in and out effortlessly. I wind up getting some of my best reflection done simply by washing dishes and staring out the window at the beautiful outdoors. Thoughts may come and go - it's how much credence I give to them that fuels them. For example, if I am upset about something and I step back, take a few deep breaths, and start to examine the real reasons for my displeasure, I am usually able to start feeling less angry almost instantly. Even though the circumstances may not have changed, the way in which I am viewing them and how I'm responding to those initial thoughts and emotions then dictates my feeling in return. Paying attention to my breath is a natural way to induce calming feelings and become centered by bringing my attention back to the present.

Do I really want to let that frustrating conversation with a co-worker ruin my day? Should I grant that person enough power over my thoughts and actions for any length of time? I'm learning more and more to be able to simply see them for what they are, including my initial reactions to them, and accept them and move on. It doesn't mean I have to suddenly agree with someone or that I don't have confrontations, but I can usually understand better why we disagree, which makes it all much less difficult, and I'm able to come up with better solutions to problems as a result of the less-muddied thinking.

There are other things that help me diffuse times of anger, frustration, sadness or other lower-level feelings that have negative energy attached. As Eckhart Tolle shares in *Stillness Speaks*, spending time with nature can also have a profound effect. Mark Nepo shares a similar sentiment in *The Exquisite Risk*. One of the biggest draws for us at our last home was the abundance of nature surrounding it, despite being in a planned development with neighbors on each side, our house backed up to a wooded area that was about a hundred yards deep and had a stream running through it. Our current home also has beautiful, wooded surroundings and wonderful parks nearby. In addition to the many trees, I have seen a wide variety of wildlife back there, including rabbits, deer, chipmunks, snakes, squirrels, coyotes, hawks and other types of birds. My favorite are the deer, especially in early Summer when the fawns start walking around with their mothers and siblings. There is something very elegant and peaceful about stepping out on the deck and watching a handful of deer casually stroll through the woods just beyond the edge of the yard.

My favorite times are first thing in the morning to watch the sun rise up above the trees, shooting rays of light through the branches and leaves until it is overhead and warms the day. The birds are singing and the dew glistens. It helps me appreciate life and its inherent beauty even more. Another favorite is standing at the grill on the back deck, preparing food for dinner, where I get a 180 degree view of nature, which is sometimes highlighted by my kids playing in the backyard. I also love the end of the day as the sun is setting. Things are quieting down, beautiful colors appear, the stars gradually begin to pop into the sky, the moon rises and occasionally a planet like Venus comes into view. Staring up at the night sky has always been a magical experience for me.

Taking walks through nature is equally soothing, as it combines a bit of physical activity and provides more dimension to things, although I confess I don't take the time to do this nearly as often as I should. However, a close approximation for me is playing golf. Although I'm not great, I'm good enough to really enjoy it and play with most people, and have settled into a mindset on the course of not getting too upset when I hit bad shots and to really enjoy being out on the course. Getting ready to tee off on many holes is a thing of beauty in itself, providing a lot of space, green grass and trees, and especially when there are streams or ponds in view as well. Some additional experiences that have been most memorable include walking through beautiful gardens at places such as the Biltmore Manner in North Carolina and Gibbs Gardens here in Georgia. One of my dreams someday is to have a ton of land with a lot of these beautiful elements.

Another outlet for me is art. To me, art is many things. It is being able to create something with expression and meaning. The main art form I turn to is writing. I write a lot, both for work and pleasure, but it is the writing I do when I feel inspired to share something that is what is most meaningful to me. There are innumerable methods of expression that can be considered art aside from the most commonly included ones, and all of them are valid, not for how other people perceive it, but for the creator of it. I love architecture as well, and enjoy coming up with home plans in my head, sketching them out on paper, or visualizing hardscape creations in my backyard. There are many other things I do that I feel have an artistic angle, such as simple home improvement projects, cooking with my wife or for my family, doodling while daydreaming, creating websites, and even building things out of blocks or Legos with my kids, doing voice impressions and singing or dancing with them. It all produces a feeling on a different plane for me, free from worry or hassle, and not being worried about what other people might think. It is blissful.

Finding ways to channel away the stress of life and replacing it with some sense of community, creation or accomplishment is like an exponential benefit, because I'm building up my reserves of positive memories and good feelings in addition to flushing out and letting go of the negative ones. Learning to place more emphasis on these things also helps to overpower the negativity bias that is inherent to daily life for most people, as evidenced by the news headlines that carry messages of the day's tragedies or conflicts. I believe we all have to have ways of purging the negative attention that otherwise produces worry, fear, anger or sadness.

8. FUEL FOR GROWTH

Several years ago, I attended a speaking event and book signing for Glennon Doyle. It was for her first book, *Carry On, Warrior: Thoughts on Life, Unarmed.* Leslie was friends with Glennon's sister, Amanda, back in college at the University of Virginia, who had since left her job as a lawyer to help manage Glennon's budding career as a speaker, writer and activist. They were in Atlanta at the Carter Library, and pretty much every seat in the auditorium was full. Oh, and I was one of only three guys in there, with one of the other ones being her husband at the time. Something really struck me in that event - the fact that Glennon openly communicated about her struggles and her ups and downs in daily life, and that she was the epitome of empathy and acceptance. I watched and listened as many women bravely shared their personal struggles as well after Glennon opened it up for questions and comments from the audience, and had to fight back the tears in myself because of the level of total acceptance in the room. Everyone who felt flawed outside of the room felt like they had a group to belong to in that room, and Glennon carried that flag of belonging and acceptance.

Glennon then went on to write another book, which was a memoir called *The Love Warrior*. In it she revealed that her husband had been unfaithful, and that she was going to recommit to her marriage. She went on Oprah and became an even bigger success. Except, as later revealed, she wound up falling in love with USA women's soccer legend Abby Wambach. She eventually divorced her husband and married Abby. She wound up losing some of her very Christian fan base by announcing her love for another woman, but eventually gained many more fans for her brave display of openness and honesty. Glennon has another book coming out called *Untamed*, which already hit bestseller lists on preorders alone. Even though most of Glennon's messages and activities are geared toward women, what I am most encouraged by is her recognition of the evolution of life, her devotion to sharing messages of love and acceptance despite imperfections we all have, and her non-profit foundation, Together Rising, that helps raise money for various social causes. She has transcended from being a "mommy blogger" into an activist and a force for good.

For me, all of this boils down to being one big learning experience and allowing the perfected chaos of life to simply continue as it will, with or without me, and to positively influence its path through me to the best of my ability. I am able to gather the things together, organize them and use them in a way that is intended to keep me moving forward and growing as well as enhance the lives of those around me. Each time I've been able to overcome some sort of setback, I feel like I have more clarity on what I need to do next. I feel like I'm learning how to have a more fulfilling life, from my family and my work interests, to serving humanity in some form and experiencing spiritual growth. I feel like I have faith in the Universe as long as my intentions are good and I'm willing to face down my fears and reconnect with life.

There are a couple applicable quotes for me about dealing with uncertainty and the fear of the unknown. One is from Pema Chödrön, where she says, "*When we resist change, it's called suffering. But when we can completely let go and not struggle against it, when we can embrace the groundlessness of our situation and relax into its dynamic quality, that's called enlightenment.*" I found that I had to start listening more to what I am drawn to - not just attracted, but compelled to move toward, even if I don't know why yet or can't explain it, to find my next calling. While that seems to be more spiritual in nature, another quote from Jonathan Fields addresses it in a slightly different way in his book *Uncertainty: Turning Fear and Doubt into Brilliance*, where he wrote, "*fear of judgment stifles our ability to embrace uncertainty and as part of that process delivers a serious blow to our willingness to create anything that hasn't already been done and validated."* These speak to me when I think about how there are times where I still feel completely lost, and then the next moment inspiration or chance conversation leads to new opportunities for growth and connection.

Recognition of some of these things within myself, while paying closer attention to what I feel I'm drawn toward the most, has led me to start taking some steps in a bit of a different direction.

At the end of 2018 I started a YouTube channel because I felt I wanted to share some things on videos, and I challenged myself to finish 52 videos in a year. In my first video, I tried to make that case that if I never started then I'd never get there, and the internal anguish I'd cause myself over *not* starting would be much worse than any potential ridicule. I'm also a big believer in the concept of a minimum valuable product (MVP), which is starting with something that is workable rather than waiting for something that is perfect. I now prefer to make changes and improvements along the way instead of not taking the next step, whereas that was definitely not always the case in the past, as I failed to keep taking those next steps.

I didn't quite make it to the full 52 videos, but I think I hit 40 during the 12-month period, and I continue to share bits of myself and thoughts as often as I remember to. With that I really took a major leap forward in opening myself up to being extremely vulnerable publicly again, and this book takes it much further. My plan is to do something good and have a lasting positive impact on as wide a sphere of influence as possible, in whatever direction that takes me or I feel called to follow.

During the spring and summer of 2019, I worked with a friend to create *We Are All People: A Children's Book About Tolerance.* I had wanted to do a children's book, or a series of them, for several years, but was afraid to. Plus, I can't draw. Even though I'm a better artist than I am a dancer, that's really not saying much at all. However, I remembered an old acquaintance I met before I moved away from Oklahoma. A guy named Randy owned the tattoo shop I had visited. I had chosen some Eastern characters that were supposed to represent the words *freedom* and *prosperity*, though in reality I have no idea if that's what they say or what language they're in. Nonetheless, when I was going through my divorce back in 2011 and had just bought a new car, I decided I was going to get this tattoo. Although Randy owned the shop, he didn't actually do the work on me, but he and I sat and talked for a while about life and politics and spirituality and recovery, and it was real. We connected. Before I moved I went in to see him again just to chat, and had another deeper conversation about life. From there we stayed in touch mainly via Facebook, and one day he started posting some pictures of paintings he was starting to do of various musicians. I sent him a note and said I wanted to get one of Tom Petty for my dad for his birthday, because he was a big fan. I also got one of Willie Nelsen for my wife. He graciously granted my request.

After I received the paintings, I asked Randy if he would be willing to do the drawings for the children's book idea I had, and after we had a phone conversation, he agreed to help me. Despite being an amazingly talented artist who could draw anything, he confessed he had never done *this* type of drawing before, and put an intense amount of pressure on himself. I tried to reassure him that I would love whatever he came up with, and after several months, he finally delivered a picture for each line in the book, plus a couple extra. His main motivation was the sentiment the book shared, and wanting to spread positive, inclusive messages to young people, especially to combat the intolerant bullying that he had born witness to and even experienced throughout his life.

I published the book on Amazon and some friends and family members picked up some copies. I donated some to my kids' schools, and Leslie even shared it as a secret reader one day in Rhett's kindergarten class. I've read it to my kids many times, and some neighbors have shared that they've read it to their kids as well. I had written the words in about an hour in a spurt of inspiration one day, and I hope the message resonates with people who read it. I recorded a video of me reading it as well, which is available on YouTube for anyone to see for free. Maybe someday it will get into more hands and people will want to continue sharing it with others.

Continuing on with wanting to share messages, during the summer of 2019 I decided to start a podcast, as I've enjoyed speaking and audio stuff more than video, because there is a bit more of a free flow for me when there isn't the consideration of a camera being present. I wound up calling it the *Support For Guys Podcast.* The initial idea came as I consumed content via books, videos and other podcasts and found myself looking for something that encouraged regular guys like me to talk more openly about issues, thoughts, feelings, etc. that have deeper meaning in life, and to do so without judgment from one another. There were some great resources available that were religiously themed, spiritually centered, specific to business and financially driven, but none that really fit what I was looking for consistently. I wasn't really looking to develop master or create any type of seven figure funnel system, but instead have meaningful conversation that helped improve my life and contributed to helping improve the lives of others as well.

Something that I had read in *The Mask of Masculinity: How Men can Embrace Vulnerability, Create Strong Relationships, and Live Their Fullest Lives* by Lewis Howes, also stuck with me. He opened up about being sexually abused as a boy, and that when he started having honest and real conversations with guy friends about past traumas, relationship problems and other things in life, they responded positively by opening up as well and sharing their own struggles.

They were able to have meaningful connection and supportive dialogue, which is something that most guys don't often have with each other.

If I'm being totally honest with myself, I have to admit that I've not made enough effort to have a strong relationship with my brother. He is four and half years older than I am and we have had very different paths growing up and through our adult life. We've each had our highs and lows, and we haven't always been very present for each other, yet we're the only siblings, and I know that I need to make more of an effort to spend time with him and his family as well.

I have tried to be more open about daily things with others, including friends and colleagues, and have found that most people want to get past the surface communication or social veneer and have a deeper connection with others, even guys. I have also found that when it first appears to backfire and seemingly creates a rift or a problem, then the actual result is that I get steered away from unhealthy or unwanted relationships or situations and onto a path of healthier, more positive ones with people who share similar desires of connection.

So, I started talking into a microphone on my computer about things that were on my mind and topics that came up in daily interactions with others. Through the small audience thus far, the feedback has been well received, even if limited. I have been able to interact and reconnect with old friends and classmates, and garner some interest in participation.

What I enjoy about the format is that I'm able to talk more freely on subjects and explore the topics a little further. It is also continuing to be a liberating experience to have another outlet for expression, and through some of this the stinging feeling of being exposed to the elements lessens, and I feel more encouraged to continue.

What I would like to see happen is for it to grow into a longer discussion each week with different guests, and blossom into support group meetings for guys online and in real life where they can have a safe, judgment-free space to talk about issues we face in our lives and find resources for help. I think that we need a system like this with a humanistic approach for helping men to help each other and have a more caring outlook on the world as a whole rather than only trying to dominate, control or fight, literally or figuratively. I have this vision of a weekend-long retreat at a golf resort where guys can enjoy some activities, network, bond, and listen and learn through workshops and speakers to help enhance their lives and figure out ways they can contribute positively to the world. I feel that the more we can teach guys to be open and express their love and appreciation for life, that we can cultivate a more attuned generation that reduces many of the male-driven social problems we now face. This also helps to raise more loving, confident children and to share the power and control equally with women, as a balance of masculine and feminine energy is sorely needed, in my opinion.

I feel like there is so much more that can be done with this, well beyond a podcast and some meetings or events. I think a conscious movement for men is warranted to help quell some of the unrest we currently see, especially around religious and political differences. We don't have to agree, but we can be more kind and conscious of one another. Episode #7 of the podcast was titled *Kindness Isn't Just Fluff*, and talked about all of the benefits to oneself and others for being kind. Citing some personal experiences and great scientific tidbits from RandomActsOfKindness.org, such as reduced stress and more pleasure, this is one of the pillars of creating a better life.

Building on the kindness then, I have also identified that I would like to give back more in some way. While we do what we can or remember to do in terms of donating items and money to charities and people in need each year, I feel like my contributions could be much more substantial in some way. Additionally, it is frustrating when I have to choose between one charity or another sometimes, when both may be equally deserving. Out of that frustration, I had an idea one day more than a year ago to start a new non-profit. This one, called GivingCommunity.org, would serve multiple purposes. First, it is a curator of as many charities as possible for people to find and figure out how they would like to help, whether through sharing their messages, giving money directly or donating time, goods or services. The second primary function, and what sets it apart from some others, is that it will have sort of non-profit indexes, or charity buckets, that would distribute funds to multiple other charities in that same category. For example, if I wanted to donate $100 to childhood illnesses, then a portion of that money would be given to each non-profit selected for that particular category. This way people can donate to *causes* of their choice and know that many well-deserving organizations in that category will each receive some funding, and when multiple people are doing the same thing, then the donations can really add up. Even smaller charities that may be lesser-known, but not any less deserving of help, get the vital fuel they need to continue doing their good works as well.

EPILOGUE

I believe we're all trying to do the best we can with the experience and knowledge we have, and within the boundaries or circumstances we find ourselves in.

I don't know what the future holds, but I do know that I can try to help make it better for others as well as myself by being kind, honest and loving as much as I am able to. I know that there will be connections lost along the way, but also many more meaningful connections made. I also know that I am a flawed person who will keep making plenty of mistakes, and that hopefully I will continue to learn from them.

The following collection of eleven principles to live by is something I have sort of decided for myself that I want to work on in my life, and also to encourage in my children as they grow. There is no particular order or rank of importance, and surely it will evolve over time, as does everything else.

1. Be inclusive - interact with others. Smile, wave, shake hands, participate, hold doors open, strike up a conversation with a stranger. By helping others feel like they matter and belong, I also feel a sense of belonging.

2. Attempt to see the world through the eyes of others, not for comparison, but instead for empathy and compassion. I believe we can learn a lot from each other when we are willing to look.

3. Learn to let go of the past and not to focus too much on previous failures, losses or battles. Forgive people who I felt have wronged me. Learn from my mistakes. Stay in the current moment by developing more resilience.

4. Follow my dreams. I write down my goals each year, and then often break them down by month and by week. I try to set some lofty annual goals in the areas of health/wellness, family, work (accomplishments as well as income) and other personal goals, including ones that may take several years to work toward. At the same time, I have to remind myself that not accomplishing them does not make me a failure, it's the pursuit that is exciting for me.

5. Try to focus on the positives rather than negatives in life. I consider myself an eternal

optimist, and the more positivity I can put my attention on, the more I will attract in return and experience around me through a higher frequency or vibration.

6. Get out and experience nature. Whether it's just taking a walk, having a garden or taking care of some animals, I try to notice the beauty that all living things possess. Fresh flowers, a chipmunk running across the yard, or the smell of a tea olive tree.

7. Find time and space for quiet reflection and meditation. For me, this comes in many forms, such as sitting or lying down for silent or guided meditations, mindful walks, going for a drive, and even things such as doing dishes, taking a shower or preparing a meal. I also receive great benefit from writing.

8. Cherish friends and family and cultivate more meaningful relationships. Connection is essential, and there are no closer connections than with those whom I love and care for the most. This simple statement cannot be emphasized enough.

9. Adopt an attitude of gratitude and humility. Be thankful for the things, people and experiences I do have instead of complaining about or comparing what I don't have.

10. Apply the Golden Rule and treat others as I would want them to treat me or someone I love. Be polite, tolerant, accepting and rid myself of judgmental thoughts and actions as much as possible, allow them to pass when they are present and forgive myself when I fail to do so.

11. Look at the moon, stars and visible planets when I can, in awe, as a reminder of how vast our universe is. It helps me to remember to let go of the small problems of daily life and embrace the experience of living.

As I finished this up, a popular thing going around social media was the "10 year challenge" of posting pictures from today compared to ten years ago. Looking back, ten years ago is really when I began this particular phase of my journey, this transformational period that leads to what, I don't know yet, but I feel this shift within me is stemming from an accumulation of the experiences I've had over the last decade or more. Maybe 2020 and beyond will bring more clarity for me.

Countless times I have found myself wondering what my life would be like if my parents hadn't gotten involved in Scientology, or if I had stayed in college, or if I would have done something else differently. But then I have to ask if I would want anything really different from the way it is today. That answer is simple - NO - I have a wonderful life now with amazing people and experiences that I wouldn't trade and couldn't imagine living without. Had I not felt the gaping wound of disconnection, I doubt I would have recognized the real value of being truly connected. And by that answer, I am affirming to myself that everything I have been through was precisely there to lead to me where I am today. All of it unfolded just as it needed to, and for that I am forever grateful.

Going forward, I want to continue to explore deeper connections in each way - with my wife and children, my extended family and friends, other people, plants and animals, art and music, mountains and valleys, oceans and plains - the universe as it can be known according to me. I plan to aim for a meaningful and fulfilling life, regardless of what each day brings, and not to lose hope when times are especially difficult.

Working through the dichotomy of trying to do something significant, yet realize my actual insignificance in the span of time, is perhaps my biggest daily struggle. Focusing more on trying to be truly present for things I do and people I'm with is a start.

ABOUT THE AUTHOR

Lucas Catton is a consultant, writer, publisher, entrepreneur and strategist who works with individuals and businesses to help them achieve their goals. He is currently the CEO of Catton Communications Corp. and Advanced Recovery Resources, LLC. For more information, visit LucasCatton.com

REFERENCES

Tutu, Desmond. *The Book of Forgiving: The Fourfold Path for Healing Ourselves and Healing Our World.* (HaperOne, March 2014)

Grant, Bridget F. Ph.D, and Dawson, Deborah A. Ph.D. *The National Epidemiologic Survey on Alcohol and Related Conditions.* https://pubs.niaaa.nih.gov/publications/arh29-2/74-78.htm

Kung Fu Panda. Screenplay by Aibel, Jonathan and Berg, Glenn. (DreamWorks Animation, June 2008)

Singer, Michael. *The Surrender Experiment: My Journey Into Life's Perfection.* (Harmony, Jun 2015)

Wright, Lawrence. *Going Clear: Scientology, Hollywood and the Prisoner of Belief.* (Vintage, Kindle edition, Jan 2013)

TonyOrgeta.org

MikeRindersBlog.org

The Lancet Psychiatry: "Childhood bullying has worse effects on mental health in young adulthood than being maltreated" https://www.eurekalert.org/pub_releases/2015-04/tl-tlp042415.php

Boone, Christian. "Judge imposes harsh sanctions on Norcross drug treatment facility" https://www.ajc.com/news/local/judge-imposes-harsh-sanctions-norcross-drug-treatment-facility/juxDSJ3SQbAT3eARGNJ5SL/ (Atlanta Journal & Constitution, Nov, 2012)

Frankl, Viktor. *Man's Search for Meaning.* (Beach Press reprint June 2006, orig. 1946 in German)

MacTaggart, Lynn. *The Bond: How to Fix Your Falling-Down World.* (Atria Books, June 2012)

Lakhiani, Vishen. "3 Ways Science Now Proves That Nobody Is Insignificant On This Planet" https://blog.mindvalley.com/tom-chi/ (Mindvalley, Feb 2018)

"Bell Prize goes to scientists who proved 'spooky' quantum entanglement is real" https://phys.org/news/2017-08-bell-prize-scientists-spooky-quantum.html (University of Toronto, Aug 2017)

Schroeder, Michael O. "The Physical and Mental Toll of Being Angry All the Time" *https://health.usnews.com/wellness/mind/articles/2017-10-26/the-physical-and-mental-toll-of-being-angry-all-the-time* (Us News & World Report, Oct 2017)

Sachdeva, Darpan. "When you know better, You do better" – The life impacting lesson Oprah learnt from Maya Angelou. *http://www.nobelthoughts.com/2017/03/04/when-you-know-better-you-do-better-the-life-impacting-lesson-oprah-learnt-from-maya-angelou/* (Nobelthoughts.com, Mar 2017)

Brené Brown. *Rising Strong: How the Ability to Reset Transforms the Way We Live, Love, Parent, and Lead.* (Random House Trade Paperbacks; Reprint edition, April 2017)

Cain, Susan. *Quiet: The Power of Introverts in a World That Can't Stop Talking*

https://sites.psu.edu/aspsy/2014/04/13/our-need-to-belong/

https://www.astrology.com/article/1111-sacred-synchronicity.html

Kabat-Zinn, Jon. *Full Catastrophe Living (Revised Edition): Using the Wisdom of Your Body and Mind to Face Stress, Pain, and Illness.* (Bantam; Revised, Updated edition, Sept 2013)

Kabat-Zinn, Jon. *Wherever You Go, There You Are: Mindfulness Meditation in Everyday Life.* (Hachette Books; 10 edition, Jan 2005)

Santorelli, Saki. *Heal Thyself: Lessons on Mindfulness in Medicine.* (Harmony; Reprint edition,Mar 2000)

Hansen, Rick. *Resilient: How to Grow an Unshakable Core of Calm, Strength and Happiness.* (Harmony, Mar 2018)

Chödrön, Pema. *Living Beautifully: with Uncertainty and Change.* (Shambhala; Reprint edition, May 2019)

Fields, Jonathan. *Uncertainty: Turning Fear and Doubt into Brilliance.* (Portfolio; Reprint edition Nov 2012)

Tolle, Eckhart. *Stillness Speaks.* (New World Library, Aug 2003)

Nep, Mark. *The Exquisite Risk.* (Harmony; Reprint edition Feb 2006)

Howes, Lewis. *The Mask of Masculinity: How Men can Embrace Vulnerability, Create Strong Relationships, and Live Their Fullest Lives.* (Rodale Books; Review copy edition, Oct 2017)

"The Science of Kindness" - https://www.randomactsofkindness.org/the-science-of-kindness

Made in the USA
Columbia, SC
13 January 2020

86752797R00090